INVESTING
FOR
RETIREMENT

ROBERT HARWOOD

INVESTING
FOR
RETIREMENT

The Ultimate Guide to Not Outliving Your Money

STRATEGIES THAT CAN HELP YOU

KEEP IT SIMPLE
KEEP IT SAFE

Published by Advantage, Charleston, South Carolina.
Member of Advantage Media Group.

ADVANTAGE is a registered trademark and the Advantage colophon is a trademark of Advantage Media Group, Inc.

Printed in the United States of America.

ISBN: 978-159932-298-8
LCCN: 2012956251

This publication is designed to provide accurate and authoritative information in regard to the subject matter covered. It is sold with the understanding that the publisher is not engaged in rendering legal, accounting, or other professional services. If legal advice or other expert assistance is required, the services of a competent professional person should be sought.

Advantage Media Group is proud to be a part of the Tree Neutral® program. Tree Neutral offsets the number of trees consumed in the production and printing of this book by taking proactive steps such as planting trees in direct proportion to the number of trees used to print books. To learn more about Tree Neutral, please visit **www.treeneutral.com**. To learn more about Advantage's commitment to being a responsible steward of the environment, please visit **www.advantagefamily.com/green**

Advantage Media Group is a leading publisher of business, motivation, and self-help authors. Do you have a manuscript or book idea that you would like to have considered for publication? Please visit **www.advantagefamily.com** or call **1.866.775.1696**

Table of Contents:

Note from the Author

As a veteran, I am sensitive to helping take care of those who sacrificed so much on our behalf. The proceeds from this book will be donated to causes that support our veterans, such as the Care Coalition for Special Operations and the Children of Fallen Heroes Foundation. These non-profit foundations and many others are supporting our troops by providing financial assistance to returning veterans, those injured by war, and the children of our fallen warriors. These brave service members and their families have sacrificed so much to help keep our great country great. It is important that we honor them and show them the support they deserve in their time of need.

– Robert Harwood

Disclaimer

The information in this book is created from the opinions of the author and is not intended as tax, investment or legal advice. The decision of how to invest and what to invest in should be made in conjunction with a competent financial professional. While the methods of investments and the theory described in this book are believed to be effective, there is no guarantee that the methods will be profitable or successful. The hypothetical illustrations referred to herein are simplified for discussion purposes and may not be applicable or appropriate for you. We recommend that you seek the counsel of a competent tax, legal, and financial advisor as applies to your particular situation. Discussions pertaining to tax treatment simply reflect our understanding of current tax laws as they apply to the subject at hand. Tax laws are subject to change. All rates quoted are hypothetical. Any guarantees associated with annuity products are contingent upon the claims-paying ability of the issuing insurance company and upon your abiding by the terms of the contract. The title of this book is not meant to imply a guarantee.

The author does not assume any responsibility for a loss and/or damages to persons, relationships, investments, or property arising out of or related to any use of the material contained in this book.

This book and the information contained herein shall not constitute an offer to sell or the solicitation of an offer to buy, nor shall there be any sale of securities in any State in which such offer, solicitation or sale would be unlawful prior to registration or qualification under the securities laws of any such state.

Any issue or recommendation contained in this book may not be suitable for all investors. The information provided is subject to change.

Preface

I have been a financial advisor for many years and have had the opportunity to assist hundreds of people with their financial needs. What I am seeing now with the new investors that I meet with is very different from previous years. Not only have the markets changed, but financial advisors and the financial products they are recommending are very different now as well. I see fewer and fewer advisors providing advice, and more and more simply selling financial products. I see financial products being packaged and sold as if just one account can fit everyone's needs: target-date funds, allocation models, and variable annuities, to name a few. The financial services industry is becoming commoditized, packaged in a way that is very efficient and cost-effective for the financial firms, and designed to maximize their profitability. Is this really right for you, the investor?

This is a trying period in history, and it will take great knowledge and a good team to successfully navigate through what is being called a "Perfect Storm." I have written this book to help people like you understand the importance of getting sound financial advice and taking the time to build a financial plan that can give you the potential to weather any storm. Whether you are comfortable financially or struggling, retired or approaching retirement, there are many investment factors that, if not properly addressed, may rob you of your retirement dreams. This book will help you determine where your current financial plan could fail, and will show you how to build a plan that will help keep you on the right financial path. It will guide you through the process of building your financial "house," and show you how to protect yourself from the many "money snatchers" that may rob you of your financial security: things like inflation, the escalating costs of health care, higher taxation, and a continued bad stock market. It will show you how to apply Murphy's Law to your portfolio and to address the possible bad things that may occur during your lifetime. Not only does this book show you how to arrange your finances in very simple-to-understand and easy-to-follow terms. It will also help to arm you with the knowledge you will need to pick the best advisors and to monitor your progress toward meeting your financial goals. Americans need a better way to invest and to learn about their choices without bias. They need to have the tools and knowledge to feel confident that they are investing their money prudently. This book will help take fear and greed out of the equation, and provide guidance towards a more secure financial future.

o n e

THE PERFECT STORM

The Perfect Storm

Americans are faced with unprecedented challenges. We just went through what many have called the "Perfect Storm": a meltdown of the financial markets. Even though the stock market has recovered from its low, many issues still remain, such as a huge and growing federal deficit, political uncertainty, and baby boomers leaving the workforce in record numbers and going on Social Security. How do you ensure that you will have the money you need to support yourself in what will hopefully be a long and enjoyable retirement? Where is the best place to invest, and how do you find the right advisor to guide you through this financial maze?

I believe that as a nation we have never faced so many problems, not just internally, but on a worldwide basis. Compounding the problems, we not only have an aging population, but that aging population will live significantly longer than previous generations, and they will consume more health care dollars than ever before. We have a large number of people dependent on government assistance, bringing more stress to an already overburdened system. American workers face significantly more economic competition from our foreign neighbors than we have ever had before while many of our jobs have been transferred overseas. We have gone from being the world's greatest lender and exporter to the world's largest debtor and importer. It seems like we no longer manufacture goods for other nations; we don't even manufacture what we consume ourselves. I believe that "Made in America" once meant quality and pride. There just aren't a whole lot of goods "Made in America" anymore.

Our government has amassed an enormous deficit, that is still growing. There is no doubt that the federal government needs to change its spending habits. Until this occurs and our government gets their financial house in order, Americans must learn how to protect their financial reserves through what may be a difficult economic period. I believe that with the exception of the Great Depression, there hasn't been a more challenging time for investors and retirees. One of the keys to creating financial security is to first identify the threats to your savings—things like inflation, taxes, poor investment choices—and then build a plan that addresses them.

Personally, I am optimistic about the future and truly believe we will find a solution for all these concerns, but it will take time for our country to get its financial house in order. During this period, we must not lose sight of our own personal financial goals, and we must protect ourselves and loved ones from the many threats that may derail our financial future. There are ways to help keep your money healthy through these tough economic times. However, the answer certainly is not what many people have chosen to do: sit on the sidelines and do nothing. Sometimes procrastination can be our worst enemy. Colin Powell, one of our great generals and leaders, said, "The inability to make a decision has cost our country much more than any wrong decision ever made." After you have finished this book, apply the knowledge you've learned to your finances. Get professional advice, and make sure you get your questions answered so that you may chart a better course.

Prior to becoming a financial planner and investment advisor representative, I received invaluable training as a military and commercial pilot. I flew jets for almost ten years in the Air Force and then went on to become a commercial airline pilot flying internationally for a major airline. As pilots, we were trained to consider every problem we might encounter during a flight and how to handle an emergency, no matter how improbable it might be. We went to work assuming it would be a good day, but we were prepared just in case the flight did not go as planned. A good example is the US Airways flight that ran into a flock of birds on takeoff out of New York and was forced to land in the Hudson River. I am sure "Sully" Sullenberger, the captain of that flight, did not go to work that day planning to land in the Hudson, but lo and behold, there he was literally "up the river." Captain Sullenberger and his copilot are heroes because they showed great judgment and skill. However, had it not been for the fact that they trained for such an event, although it was highly improbable, the outcome might have been very different. Pilots spend hours in the simulator learning to handle any emergency, and then "go to the line" expecting a smooth flight. They are prepared for the unexpected, just in case. As a passenger on an airplane, you may take great comfort knowing that your pilots are trained to handle any emergency, no matter how improbable it may be. This is the best way to approach your retirement planning as well.

How much better would you sleep at night if you knew your finances were invested in a way that would help weather a financial meltdown, whether or not it actually occurred? Build your portfolio in such a manner that if something does go wrong, you will be prepared and it will not derail your retirement. Hope for the best, but always plan for the worst. Wouldn't you feel better knowing that your financial plan was designed to address the different problems that you might encounter, such as stock market instability and high inflation? Don't let Murphy's Law negatively affect your retirement dreams.

I am sure many of you are familiar with the story about Captain Edward Murphy and what has become known as Murphy's Law.[1] Captain Murphy was an engineer who was involved in an Air Force project to test how much deceleration a person could withstand in an airplane crash. When the technician working on Murphy's project wired all of the sensors for the test backward, Captain Murphy was heard muttering his famous phrase, "If anything can go wrong, it will go wrong."

Now let's apply this line of thinking to your retirement plan. Ask yourself, "What could go wrong and break my plan?" And then ask yourself whether you, or your financial advisor, have taken the time to address those issues. If the answer is "no," or "I'm not sure," then you may need to make some changes. The consequences of not addressing these items can be catastrophic. Who wants that kind of uncertainty in their life? This book will help you identify the weak points in your plan and provide you with invaluable lessons on how to invest in these challenging times.

Thinking of all that can go wrong while there is still time to do something about it is an important exercise. Apply Murphy's Law to your retirement plan and you may just feel a little more confident. No one knows what the future holds, but it may be a tough few years ahead.

By the way, Murphy had a second law: "Left to themselves, things tend to go from bad to worse."

---

1   "Applying Murphy's Law To Retirement", *Forbes*, Liz Davidson, 2010.

INVASION OF THE MONEY SNATCHERS

Invasion of the Money Snatchers

You have worked hard and now it is time to retire and begin enjoying the fruits of your labor. Are you finished now? Are you all set for a long, active, and financially secure retirement? Maybe not. Most of the people that I have met in my practice, with or without the help of a financial advisor, haven't really taken time to think through their goals and to build a financial plan that can help protect them from the many events that could derail their retirement—things like high inflation, unexpected health care costs, or just a continued bad stock market. There are a lot of problems you may encounter during your retirement and you need to address these potential threats in your plan. I call these threats the "money snatchers," and they can be lethal.

THE MONEY SNATCHERS: WHAT ARE THEY?

The seven most common "money snatchers" are:

1. The risk of living a long time and running out of money— *longevity risk.*
2. A continued bad stock (securities) market—*market risk.*
3. Having your life savings eroded by inflation—*inflation risk.*
4. Paying high and maybe unnecessary taxes—*poor tax planning.*
5. The escalating cost of health care—*risk of a major health related event that is not covered by insurance.*
6. Poor or inappropriate financial advice.

7. The internal costs of your investments, such as brokerage commissions and mutual fund fees. (I have personally seen many cases where an investor's stockbroker or financial advisor is making more off of their accounts than they are.)

The possibility of outliving your savings or suffering losses due to high inflation, market volatility, taxes, high health care costs, and high fees are the true money snatchers.

The good news is that for every risk there is a compensating solution. If you want to protect your portfolio you need to think about the risks you are exposed to and address all of the risks. This is how you create true financial security by addressing any issues that can derail your retirement. A lot of people see the stock market as one of the greatest risks to their savings, but that isn't so. The stock market is just one of many tools available to you to beat the money snatchers. When utilized properly, the stock market is an invaluable tool for creating financial security. Avoiding the stock market altogether is not the answer. Instead, you need to sit down with a financial professional and ask that person to help you to identify your risks and guide you to the appropriate solutions.

Your money will provide for your quality of life in retirement, good or bad. If you want to put the odds of having a long and enjoyable retirement in your favor, you must have a plan that addresses all of these money snatchers: market volatility, taxes, inflation, health care, longevity, and the fees associated with your investments. These money snatchers can silently rob your financial future.

In future chapters we will discuss each of these money snatchers, as well as what you can do to protect your retirement from them. Your true financial security will come from addressing the threats to your retirement and building a plan that has a high probability of success, regardless of market conditions.

three

INFLATION: THE SILENT RETIREMENT KILLER

Inflation: The Silent Retirement Killer

It is likely that, in the not-too-distant future, we will have significantly higher taxes, lower benefits from our entitlement programs, and inflation. In this section, we will tackle inflation and what you can do to protect yourself from this retirement killer. In reality, inflation is just another tax on your savings. If not planned for, it can have a devastating effect on the long-term buying power of your money. Inflation is a very powerful money snatcher, and has the potential to negatively affect retirees more than any other group of people.

The following chart illustrates the amount of additional income you will need to keep up with inflation at a 3.1 percent annual rate.

Now	5 Years	10 Years	15 Years
$35,000	$41,168	$48,424	$57,750
$50,000	$58,812	$69,179	$83,500
$75,000	$88,219	$103,768	$125,250

Required increases in income to keep up with inflation

The chart below illustrates the difference between the tax reserves collected by our government and our national deficit in 2010. Imbalances like these can greatly impact our markets and may lead to significant inflation in the not too distant future.

Source: Office of Management and Budget 2010

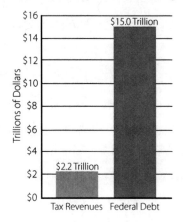

Do our government officials need to get our country's financial house in order? There is no doubt, but until they do, you need to know how to protect yourself and your family from this gigantic problem. There is a good website you can visit to learn more about our deficit and unfunded liabilities: www.usdebtclock.org. It shows the real-time numbers on our deficit and other liabilities. It is worth a visit, and it is eye opening![1]

---

1   This website is maintained by a third party and is not sponsored by nor is it verified that the content, accuracy, or opinions expressed are valid and disclaims any warranty or liability for damages associated therewith.

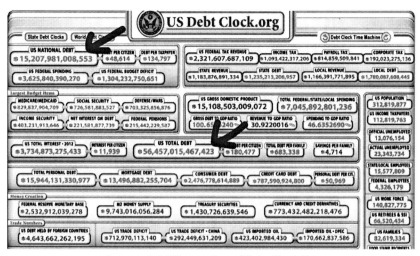

January 8, 2012 snapshot of Debt Clock.Org

One of the problems I encounter as an advisor is that too many of the people, even those using the services of a financial advisor, have not taken the time to address the threat of inflation to their retirement lifestyle. I normally offer investors the opportunity to meet with me to get a second opinion on their finances and investment accounts, and I will take the time to point out areas where there could be improvement. I will often ask them whether their current advisor has discussed inflation with them and, if so, what their advisor has done to protect them from this "stealth" tax. Most people just look at me and say, "They really haven't said anything!" Remember, you are paying your financial advisors and stockbrokers to help you protect your financial future to the greatest extent possible. Can they really do this if they don't take the time to address something as important as the effect of inflation on your savings and income? No one is immune to inflation. You have to address the prospects of high inflation in your plan as well as continued stock market volatility.

WHAT TO DO AND WHAT NOT TO DO

Let's say you are frustrated with the stock market. You are tired of losing money, so you put your money in the bank, maybe a certificate of deposit (CD) paying two percent interest. Two percent interest is a very low interest rate to earn for tying up your money. But people are still putting their money in the bank, because they are scared to death of losing money in the stock market and don't know where else to turn. So let's say you decide to put some of your money in bank CDs; are you really making money, or are you still losing? For example, if your CD is paying 2 percent and if inflation is 3 percent, how much money are you making? You are actually going backward because of buying power. You may not see it on your bank statement, but you are losing money. Although there certainly is a place and a need for bank CDs, I believe that interest rates are too low and they will typically have some form of penalty for cashing them in early. I do recommend using the bank to help you meet your needs for liquidity, but putting too much money in an account that doesn't provide much potential for growth is not something that I would do with my money. So what is a prudent investor to do?

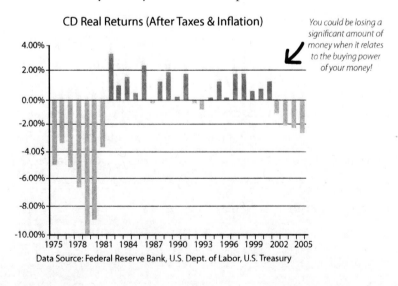

CD Real Returns (After Taxes & Inflation)

You could be losing a significant amount of money when it relates to the buying power of your money!

Data Source: Federal Reserve Bank, U.S. Dept. of Labor, U.S. Treasury

KEEPING PACE WITH INFLATION

There are many ways to keep pace with inflation. Some are safer than others. One way to keep up with inflation is to invest in things that tend to go up in price with inflation. For example, American consumers have seen significant increases in the cost of gasoline at the gas pumps over the last few years. If you want to keep up with this inflation, then you may consider owning stock in a gasoline company or elsewhere in the energy sector.[2] As gas prices go up, then presumably your investments should increase in value as well, helping you offset these costs. When you go to the grocery store and you see things getting expensive—items like bread and milk—you could choose to own investments that will offset these costs as well. Here you might want to invest in a good quality company that specializes in consumer staples.[3] As prices go up, so should your investment's value. You can do this with many of the sectors that tend to rise with inflation, such as gas, electricity, health care, and food. You have to be careful here—you want to own stock in good companies, and I prefer dividend payers in this area. You need the right amount invested for inflation protection. We will discuss how much and how to build this portion of your portfolio in future chapters.

Stocks are important, but remember they are risky, and I would recommend that you never risk any money you cannot afford to lose in the equity markets. Buying the right investments is just one of many options that are available to help protect your savings and income from the effects of inflation. For those of you who just don't

---

2 The intention of this section of the book is not to make stock and investment recommendations, it is simply to provide examples of possible investments that may help offset the effects of inflation.

3 Individual stocks are subject to company or management risk, which may not correlate.

feel comfortable with securities, there are several other inflation-protected investments for you to utilize, which may have significantly less risk than buying individual stocks. For example, there are Treasury Inflation-Protected Securities (TIPS), Inflation Protected Annuities (IPAs), Total Return Funds, and more.

TREASURY INFLATION-PROTECTED SECURITIES (TIPS)

Treasury Inflation-Protected Securities (TIPS) are a less volatile investment than buying individual stocks, and can help you stay abreast of inflation. TIPS are issued by the U.S. government and linked to the rate of inflation. They will pay a nominal rate of interest and adjust its value with the declared rate of inflation. To illustrate how TIPS work, let's return to the topic of bank CDs. Let's say you are a little nervous about the stock market and have a certain amount of money you just don't want to lose, so you put it in CDs. Following our previous example, lets say these CDs have a declared rate of interest of 2 percent per year, and a certain term during which if you take your money out early, they charge you a penalty. As we said earlier, if real inflation is 3 percent and you are earning 2 percent on your CD (Certificate of Depreciation, in this case), you are losing buying power. If inflation goes up to 5 or 6 percent, you are just losing buying power a little faster.

Now, let's instead put that same money into TIPS. For this example, assume the TIPS has a 2 percent declared rate of interest, like our CD example. The way TIPS work is they pay you their stated rate of interest (2 percent in this example) plus make an adjustment for the declared rate of inflation. So if inflation is 3 percent, then your TIPS should pay 5 percent, and if inflation increases to 5 percent in this example, the TIPS should pay 7 percent (2 percent plus the declared rate of inflation). Can you see how TIPS can help your savings stay healthy by adjusting with inflation? Now, TIPS also have their own problems. For example, if the government declares there is no inflation, as they have in the past, then your interest earned in this example will be just 2 percent. There is also the potential to have negative inflation or deflation. TIPS may not make a lot of money, but if you want to put your money away for the long term, say a year or longer, and don't want the potential for its value to be eroded by the effects of inflation, then TIPS may be a better bet than a bank CD. At least you have a fighting chance of keeping up with inflation.

TIPS can be bought without any commissions, so they are similar to CDs in this way. But TIPS are not for everyone and there is a right time and a wrong time to use them. It depends on your goals and personal situation.[4]

I have found that too many advisors have not taken the time to discuss TIPS with their clients. If TIPS may be a way for you to keep your money safe from inflation, and they can be bought without a sales charge or commission, why aren't your advisors telling you about them? Isn't it their job to help protect your financial welfare?

The following charts show stock market returns adjusted for inflation in one-, three-, and ten-year periods. The period used for all three charts is from 1926 until 2008.

---

4   TIPS can be bought from the treasury directly and have certain risks associated with this particular investment. Make sure you take the time to read the prospectus and other literature before investing in TIPS. I recommend you seek the advice of a competent financial professional to help you determine if TIPS may be right for your situation.

US Large Company Stock Returns after Inflation, 1926 to 2009

US stocks - 1 year returns after inflation

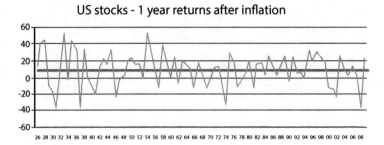

US stocks - 3 year returns after inflation

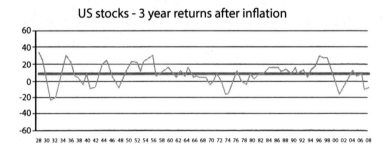

US stocks - 10 year returns after inflation

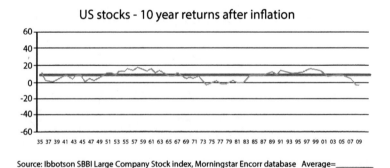

Source: Ibbotson SBBI Large Company Stock index, Morningstar Encorr database   Average=_____

Inflation is truly like a stealth tax eating away at the value of your savings. When the effects of inflation are added into the equation, has the stock market really made any money? A properly diversified plan needs to address the effects of inflation on your portfolio. The stock market may be a great place to grow your wealth; it should not be ignored or avoided, but the fact remains that many investors have not made real dollars when you factor in inflation and taxes.[5] In a later chapter we will show how to build a portfolio that will address inflation's effects and allow you the comfort of knowing you have considered this potential threat to your retirement and future quality of life.

---

5   Ibbotson, "The Stock Market Returns vs. Inflation", 2009.

four

TAXES: THE GOOD, THE BAD AND THE UGLY

Taxes: The Good, the Bad and the Ugly

If you managed your finances like the government does, you would either be bankrupt or have to work three jobs just to make ends meet. The only way they get away with it is that Uncle Sam can do something that would land you or me in jail: they can print money. Our elected officials have been financially irresponsible for too many years and have simply printed money rather than changing their bad spending habits. They have spent our country's economy into a corner and unfortunately it is not Uncle Sam's money that is being recklessly spent; it is ours. You and I and our children, and possibly grandchildren, are the ones who will have to pay for this. It seems that they are just hoping that the economy starts growing so we can grow our way out of this mess. Then they won't have to address issues like their poor spending habits.

FEDERAL GOVERNMENT SPENDING
AND YOUR TAXES

Other than growing our way out of this mess, the primary options that Uncle Sam has to deal with this enormous deficit are to either depreciate the debt away (the worst option), default on the debt (highly unlikely and ugly), or raise our taxes significantly. The answer, I believe, lies within the first and last option. The government may depreciate away some of the debt and will possibly need to significantly raise taxes on all Americans.

How much will the government have to raise taxes? I am not sure, but if you look at the following chart titled, "History of Federal

Individual Income Top Marginal Tax Rates," you will see that we have had an average tax rate of about 55-60 percent over the last 100 years. If our deficit and national debt is above average, is there any reason to assume it won't take above average tax rates to pay off an above average deficit? Will taxes more than double? I don't know, but I think it is a sure bet we will see our tax rates increase significantly in the not too distant future. Because of our government's past excesses and the constant printing of money that has gone on over recent years, they really don't have any other option but to significantly raise our taxes. In my opinion, they have spent us into a corner and will be forced to reduce our services, change our entitlement programs (Social Security, Medicare and Medicaid) and significantly increase the taxes we have to pay. It is as if you continued to charge to your credit cards until you hit your limits and then you continued spending. If you let it go on too long, it becomes very difficult to get out of debt! Below is a chart that shows historical tax rates. The higher brackets historically have averaged in the 60 percent range, and were as high as 92 percent.

History of Federal Individual Income Top Marginal Tax Rates

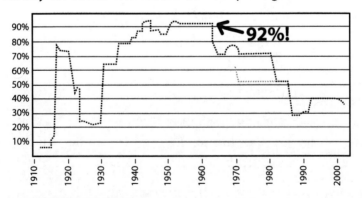

Black: Top marginal rate

Gray: Top marginal rate on earned income, if different.

Source: truthandpolitics.org, referencing IRS Statistics of Income Bulletin Pub 1136

It may take generations to pay off our debt, and the people who will do the best in the future high-tax-rate environment and suffer the least will be those who take the time to manage their taxes and have a good tax plan. **Those who don't take the time to create a tax plan may suffer the most.**

Who should you go to to get tax advice on how to manage the impact taxes have on your financial situation and how to keep them as low as possible? Should you talk to the people at a tax preparation service, or whoever prepared your tax return, or should you talk to your financial advisor? The answer is actually both. You pay each of these individuals to help you, and although your financial advisor may argue otherwise, much of the taxes you pay in retirement will come from your investments. How you invest your money and where you hold your investments (IRAs, Roths, trusts or taxable accounts) can have a significant impact on how much you will pay in taxes. Making money in the stock market is great, but it is the money you keep that really counts. Investment advice without addressing taxes is just wasteful. Based on my experience, too many people are missing opportunities that may help them reduce or avoid future taxes, and many of them have a financial advisor who has never said a word to them. Just a small savings can make a significant difference over your lifetime, and can save you from paying more than your fair share of taxes.

SHELTERING YOUR MONEY FROM UNNECESSARY TAXES: MULTIGENERATIONAL IRAs, ROTH IRAs, AND TAXES

Roth IRAs and Multigenerational IRAs are types of accounts that can help you manage your taxes and the taxes your children will have to pay on your IRAs after you pass away. First, let's talk about the difference between a traditional IRA and a Roth IRA. A traditional IRA, as well as a 401(k) and a 403(b), are tax-deferred accounts where pre-tax money is deposited. It can grow tax-deferred until the money is withdrawn. IRAs, 401(k)s, and 403(b)s are similar, with the main distinction being that you can put almost any investment in an IRA, including real estate, gold, annuities, stocks, etc. The 401(k)s and 403(b)s are company plans, and can be very limited in your investment choices. (If you want to see lists of investments that can be made in an IRA, just go to the IRS Web site, www.irs.gov, and look in publication 590.)

I like IRAs more than 401(k)s or 403(b)s because of the additional investment choices and additional flexibility they give you. For example, there are cases where you can buy rental properties and real estate holdings in your IRA. You will not normally see this option in a 401(k). Additionally, in a company plan like a 401(k) or 403(b) you have no control over your costs; you will with traditional IRAs. If you are retired and have left your retirement funds in your old 401(k) or 403(b) accounts, you may want to consider directly transferring it to your own traditional IRA. This may be very beneficial for you, and there are very few cases in which leaving your old retirement account "behind" might make sense.

Let's get back to the basics of the IRAs. As long as you do not withdraw the money from your IRA, it will remain tax-deferred. The taxes on the money in your account are deferred for your lifetime, and for your spouse, as long as your money stays in the IRA. But what happens when you withdraw money, or you die and leave your IRA or 401(k) to your kids? That's right: taxes—lots of taxes. Remember, you will be forced to start taking distributions from your IRAs and other retirement accounts when you turn 70½, and this may be at a time when tax rates are significantly higher. With the prospects of higher taxes in the not-too-distant future, it is important to address the tax ramifications of your accounts. You need to look for legal and practical ways to reduce your current and future tax liabilities. You have plenty of options. As a financial advisor, I have taken the time to study taxes and techniques to reduce the taxes my clients may have to pay. My job is to help protect their financial welfare and that is difficult to do without addressing the effects of taxation on my clients' investments and income.

MULTIGENERATIONAL IRAs

IRAs help us to build tax-deferred wealth, but I do not believe that they are good inheritance vehicles. IRAs are tax-deferred for your lifetime and your spouse's, but cannot be "rolled over" to your children's IRAs when you pass away, a common misconception. Typically, according to Ed Slott[1], a leading expert on IRAs, your children will be taxed on the entire amount of your IRA as ordinary income when they inherit. As you can imagine, this could mean a significant amount of taxes that they may have to pay. If I told you that you had to take all the money out of your IRA tomorrow, how

---

1   *The Retirement Savings Time Bomb...and How to Defuse It: A Five-Step Action Plan for Protecting Your IRAs, 401(k)s*, Ed Slott, Penguin, First edition, January 3, 2012.

would that affect your taxes? Most people wouldn't want to do it, because the tax liability could be devastating. Well, that is what might happen when you die and leave your IRAs to your children. They may have to pay taxes on the entire amount they inherit and this will be on top of their current tax liabilities. What is unfortunate is that it is all unnecessary, with the proper planning. There are effective tools available for you to protect both yourself and your children from unnecessary taxation on your IRAs. Roth IRAs may help, but another valuable tool is a Multigenerational IRA. If you don't want to invest in a Roth, at a minimum make sure you consider setting up your IRAs multi-generationally. Multigenerational IRAs do not have any negative effects on you or the account holder, nor do they cost anything to set up, or affect what or how you invest. However, they will provide your children with a chance to keep your IRAs deferred for multiple generations.[2]

Multigenerational IRAs came about almost ten years ago when the IRS finalized new regulations regarding required distributions of IRAs. Unfortunately, too many people are not aware of these rules. According to Ed Slott, about 85 percent of IRAs will fail to take full advantage of this important rule.[3] This new regulation has no effect on the account holder, but will have a significant impact on your beneficiaries when they inherit your retirement accounts. Under the old rules, children and grandchildren who inherited an IRA or a pre-tax retirement account (IRA, 401(k), 403(b), etc.) were forced

---

2   We recommend that you seek the counsel of a competent tax, legal, and financial advisor as applies to your particular situation.

3   *The Retirement Savings Time Bomb...and How to Defuse It: A Five-Step Action Plan for Protecting Your IRAs, 401(k)s*, Ed Slott, Penguin, First edition, January 3, 2012.

to pay taxes on the entire account. The distribution of the IRA had to occur from one to five years after the death of the account owner.

Under the new distribution rules, beneficiaries can take withdrawals from the "inherited" IRA over their lifetime and pay taxes only on their withdrawals. What this means is that when you pass on, your IRA stays intact, and your children pay taxes only on their distributions. A distribution table was established for inherited IRAs, and required distributions are mandatory for the beneficiaries, regardless of their ages. These new distribution rules allow the recipient of the account to spread their distributions and taxes over their individual lifetimes. According to my studies, the average IRA can remain tax deferred for up to 140 years. Can you imagine how large your IRA could grow if it remained sheltered from taxes for more than 100 years? Can you also imagine the opportunity you are missing to help your children if you do not take advantage of this new ruling? Set up properly, your IRA can be passed from generation to generation. You leave it to your children and when they pass, it goes to your grandchildren, in a tax friendly manner. This is extremely important, considering the prospect that your children will probably be paying significant taxes to get the federal deficit under control.

The length of time your IRA can remain tax-deferred is based on your age at your death and the age of the beneficiaries at the time they inherit your IRA. A $300,000 IRA that grows at an average rate of 5 percent per year can have the potential to pay out as much as $1.5 million in distributions over three generations. A knowledgeable financial advisor should be well schooled on Multigenerational IRAs and be able to assist you with this process of setting your account up. You can also find several articles and books on the subject. What a great opportunity to assist your children at a time when they may be paying sky-high taxes.

The Multigenerational IRA is one of the easiest strategies to employ to help reduce the taxes your beneficiaries will have to pay on their inheritance. There are several other wealth-transfer strategies that are quite powerful and easy to implement as well. In this book, we will focus only on the Multigenerational IRAs and Roth conversions. I suggest that if you are interested in maximizing the benefit of your legacy to your children, you should seek the advice of a competent financial professional to learn more about your options and see if they may be right for you.

ROTH IRAs

Roth IRAs are another tool to help you manage your future tax liabilities. They differ from traditional IRAs and 401(k)s. In general, with a traditional IRA or 401(k), when you put money in the account, it is pre-tax (not taxed) and it grows tax deferred. Whenever you take money out of your IRA, you will be taxed on the entire withdrawal. With Roth IRAs, the money you put in has already been taxed (post-tax money), it grows tax-free and most importantly, when you withdraw the money, it is tax-free. Farmers have a saying: "I would rather have you tax my seed than my harvest." Let's say you plant a bag of corn seed and you grow acres and acres of corn, enough to fill two trucks from your harvest. If you were the farmer, which would you prefer that the government tax, your seed or your harvest? The seed, of course! With regular IRAs and 401(k)s, the government taxes the harvest, not the seed. Each year you invested a bit of money in your retirement accounts (IRAs and 401(k)s), and over the years, the accounts increased in value, partly because the growth was tax-deferred. Over time you may have amassed a significant amount of money and "future tax liabilities" in your IRAs. When you begin taking withdrawals from your IRAs, Uncle Sam will tax that harvest, and it may be at a time when taxes are significantly higher than they are today.

With a Roth IRA, you put in after-tax money. You do not receive a tax deduction for your contributions into a Roth, but the account will grow tax-deferred. When you take distributions from your Roth account they are income-tax-free not only for you, but also income-tax-free to your beneficiaries when they inherit your account. You have paid tax on the seed, not the harvest. Roths aren't right for everyone, but it is certainly worth considering for most investors.

TO ROTH OR NOT TO ROTH?

Many of you may see the benefit of a Roth but are concerned about the taxes you will have to pay when you pull the money from your IRAs to put into your Roth accounts. The answer to whether you should use a Roth depends on several factors, including your age and the age of your spouse, your current tax bracket, and how much money you have invested in IRAs. It may be beneficial to convert some portion of your IRA to a Roth in today's relatively low tax environment. It would be difficult to imagine a case for the conversion of your entire IRA to a Roth IRA unless you are focused only on the income taxes your children will have to pay on your estate.

Remember, we are at historically low tax rates; it is likely that rates will go up significantly in the future. If you take money from your traditional IRAs and convert it into Roths, you will be locking in today's tax rates, and will not have to pay higher rates in the future. There are certain rules that apply to Roths, so you want to make sure you discuss them with your tax adviser and take the time to understand them before you open an account.

I recommend that anyone with a large balance in their IRAs take the time to have their situation analyzed for a possible Roth conversion. The idea with a Roth conversion is to convert money from your IRA to a Roth in the most tax-efficient manner. We use a program called a "Roth-Roll Out" to help us determine a tax efficient way to convert funds from a traditional IRA to a Roth. If you can convert the funds in your IRA to a Roth without significantly increasing your tax bracket, it will probably be a home run for you and your beneficiaries.

The following is a checklist of five basic items that you may want to review regarding your IRAs, to help preserve their value for yourself and future generations.

1. **Make sure you have a distribution plan for your IRAs and other retirement accounts.** How and when you take your withdrawals can have a significant affect on the taxes you will pay over your lifetime. An IRA is a great savings tool, but keep in mind that every dollar that is withdrawn will be taxed as ordinary income. Ed Slott says that IRAs are "infested" with taxes. With the prospects of higher taxes in the future, it is now more important than ever to develop a distribution plan for your IRAs. The worst thing you can do when it comes to taxes and your IRAs is to leave it up to chance and assume everything will be fine.

2. **A completed beneficiary form may not be enough.** Make sure you take advantage of the "separate accounts" rule. IRS publication 590 states, "If separate accounts with separate beneficiaries are not established, all beneficiaries' distributions will be based on the life expectancy of the oldest beneficiary." Using the separate accounts rule will

help minimize the taxes your beneficiaries will have to pay, with little to no effect on you, the IRA account holder. Take advantage of this often-overlooked rule to maximize your distributions.

3. **Work with an advisor who understands the rules and regulations governing IRAs and other retirement accounts.** Poor advice may result in IRA owners and their beneficiaries losing out on great opportunities. Too many advisors have not taken the time to learn the new distribution rules. Unfortunately, it is their clients and their clients' beneficiaries who may miss out on a great opportunity. Not only must the IRA owner meet specific guidelines to minimize the taxation on their IRAs, but also the owner's beneficiaries have requirements that must be met once the account is inherited. It is important that they are made aware of the rules they must follow. For example, they must take their first distribution from the account before December 31 in the year following the year that the IRA owner passed away. Your advisor's job is to help you protect your financial best interests; they should be available to help your beneficiaries as well. It is important to work with a financial advisor that understands the distribution rules that are associated with IRAs and retirement accounts. You don't want to miss out on the opportunity to reduce any taxation on these accounts.

4. **You are retired or have left your previous employer and you still have funds in a 401(k), 403(b), or other employer/company plan.** Many of the new distribution rules are particular to IRAs only and do not apply to 401(k) and 403(b) accounts. If you want to take advantage

of these rules you need to "roll," or directly transfer, your company retirement accounts to your own personal self-directed IRA. Rolling your company's plan to a roll-over or traditional IRA will allow you to control the cost structure of your accounts and open up your investment choices, as well as allowing you to take advantage of the new distribution rules. Company plans are designed in a manner that will keep the costs low for the company, and are not always in your best interests.

5. **If you will be relying on your IRAs and retirement accounts to support you throughout your retirement, then make sure they are invested in a way that will help you meet your retirement income needs.** Generally, as we get older we need to be "safer" with our investments, especially when it comes to the money you will need to live on. Younger investors can suffer loses and still have time to recover, but as we get older, it becomes more and more difficult to recover after a downturn in the market. Time just may not be on your side. Do not risk any more money than you can afford to lose to the stock market, and make sure you are comfortable with the way your IRAs are invested. Most peoples' retirement accounts will be providing income during their retirement years. If this is the case for you, make sure you are protecting your income and ability to provide for your retirement. I have seen too many cases where people were exposing money to the markets that they just could not afford to lose. There are many low-risk alternatives that might suit your needs and be a better choice. Make sure you are investing your

money in a manner that you are comfortable with and go enjoy your retirement.

Remember, if you don't have a plan for your taxes, Uncle Sam does.

f i v e

THE RISING COSTS OF HEALTH CARE AND WHAT YOU CAN DO

The Rising Costs of Health Care
and What You Can Do

A 2008 article in *The Wall Street Journal*[1] discusses the need for retirees to plan for the costs of long-term care. It states, "...a couple turning 65 has a 75 percent chance that one of them will need long-term care." The article explains that parents who don't plan ahead for long-term care thereby leave their children with what economists call a "negative inheritance." Basically, the term means that when the parents' savings run out due to the need for long-term care, their children *inherit* the long-term care bills.

The National Academy of Elder Law Attorneys[2] did a study comparing the risk of financial devastation brought on by long-term care with the risk of financial devastation brought on by a major automobile accident or a house fire. According to that study, the rates of risk were:

- Automobile accident: 1 out of 240 [0.4 percent]
- House fire: 1 out of 1,200 [0.08 percent]
- Long-term care: 1 out of 2 [50 percent]

Further research found that 20 percent of all people age 65 or older need help performing their normal activities of daily living (ADLs). At age 85, the estimate grows to about 50 percent. The worst-case scenario in terms of financial burden involves entering a nursing home. The odds of a person needing long-term care in a nursing home at various ages are:

---

1   "When Inheritance is Negative," *The Wall Street Journal*, Personal Finance, by Marshall Eckblad, Jan 22, 2008.

2   National Academy of Elder Law Attorneys, www.naela.prg/library, 2012.

- 45 or older: 36 percent
- 65 or older: 49 percent
- 85 or older: 56 percent

People will pay for car and home-owner's insurance, just in case they have some sort of unforeseen catastrophic event. They are insuring themselves against the possibility of an accident or house fire. As we can see from the table above, the probability of an auto accident or a house fire is significantly less then the chance of spending time in a nursing home, yet too many people have neglected addressing this potentially costly event.

No one wants to go into a nursing home, but unfortunately there is a time when statistically one out of two of us will need this level of care. You can stay healthy, exercise, and eat right, and this should help provide you with a better quality of life, but it certainly offers no guarantee against spending time in a facility or the need for some form of long-term care. To protect yourself from this cost, you don't necessarily have to buy a long-term care insurance policy; there are other alternatives available that you should evaluate as well. The one thing you should not do is just "ignore it" and assume you will deal with it when the time comes. There is a significant possibility that you will be spending money on one of these eventualities, and you need to address this contingency in your plan.

According to the Center for Retirement Research at Boston College,[3] a typical 65-year-old couple can expect to spend over their remaining lifetime $197,000, excluding nursing home care, on their medical costs. You can add another $300,000 to $500,000 to your

---

3 "Health Care Costs Drive Up the National Retirement Risk Index," Alicia H. Munnell, Mauricio Soto, Anthony Webb, Francesca Golub-Sass, and Dan Muldoon, http://globalag.igc.org/health/us/2008/costs.pdf, February 2008, IB#8-3.

projected costs for covering the care that your normal insurance will not pay if long-term care is needed.

MEDICAID, LONG-TERM CARE INSURANCE, AND THE SELF-PAY OPTION

I have heard people say that they are not worried about long-term care; if they need it, they will let the government pay for it. This is not an option that I would want to use. Do you know what you have to be to qualify for government aid (Medicaid)? Broke! Currently, to qualify for Medicaid, a single individual can have only $2,000 in financial assets[4] to his or her name. Medicaid is a program for people who cannot afford care and is, in reality, a welfare program. Another aspect to consider is that if you are on Medicaid, who is going to be determining the level and types of care you receive, you and your family or some government agency? Do you really want to be on Medicaid?

With such a high probability of your needing this type of care, your financial advisor should take time to discuss this with you. I am not saying that you need to run out and buy a long-term care (LTC) policy; there are many alternatives that are available to you to help you address these costs. With a fifty-fifty chance of needing some form of long-term care,[5] you need to make sure that your plan addresses the possibility of this need. I personally prefer to self-fund and use some form of a health care rider that can be included with

4   "Medicaid and Long Term Care for the Elderly, How to Qualify, Eligibility Requirements and Benefits, www.PayingForSeniorCare.com, 2012

5   "AARP. Beyond 50: A Report to the Nation on Independent Living and Disability," http://www.aarp.org/health/doctors-hospitals/info-11-2003/beyond_50_03__a_report_to_the_nation_on_independent_living_and_disability.html, 2003.

an Insurance or annuity account to help offset these costs. We will discuss these riders later in this chapter.

You generally have three options when it comes to medical costs associated with long-term care, assisted living, or home health care, none of which are covered by your regular health insurance

1. You pay for it yourself out of your savings: i.e., self-pay.
2. You buy an insurance policy, like long-term care insurance.
3. You let the government pay for it; i.e., Medicaid.

THE SELF-PAY OPTION

If you plan to pay for it yourself rather than buying an insurance policy, you are essentially self-insured, which means you use your money to pay the bill. So how much will you need to self-insure? In Florida, the average cost of long-term care is about $300 a day, according to a recent study released by the Kaiser Family Foundation.[6] This is for basic care; if you have Alzheimer's disease or you need specialized care, it can be significantly more. If the cost of your care, or your spouse's care, is $9,000 or more per month, how long will your money last? For some this may not be a problem, but for many it can rob them of their life's savings. Although self-pay may be the option of choice, many people simply cannot afford the cost.

LONG-TERM HEALTH CARE INSURANCE

The second option that you may have is to buy a long-term care insurance policy. This is not a bad option for some people, but it has its drawbacks. These polices can be expensive, and they normally

6 "Briefing on Long-term Care," Kaiser Family Foundation, February, 7, 2011.

will have strict limits on the benefits they pay. If you are older, ill, or have a family history of illness, you may not be insurable, or the policy can be very expensive. If you are considering long-term care insurance, normally the best time to get it is when you are in your late 50s or early 60s. The thing to be aware of if you are considering the purchase of an LTC policy is that the insurers will generally limit the daily benefit amount they pay, the number of years/months they will pay, and the total amount they will pay over your lifetime. I frequently see policies that cap benefit payments at about $340,000. So if you buy a policy and you are unfortunate enough to have to use it, you will have to begin picking up the tab after you exceed these limits.

HEALTH CARE RIDERS—ANOTHER OPTION

I am sure you don't want to go on Medicaid, and I certainly don't want to be on this welfare program, but guess what? The government doesn't want you on Medicaid either. Medicaid is a very expensive program for the government, and it is one of the key areas where our government is looking to cut costs.

In 2006, as part of the Pension Protection Act, Congress enacted an incentive to keep you off of the Medicaid program and to create incentives to get you to "self-pay" for your long-term care costs. Inside the Pension Protection Act is a section that introduces health care riders.[7] A health care rider is an "attachment" to a life insurance or annuity policy that adds an additional benefit to the policyholder. It assists you, the policyholder, in self-paying your costs for long-term care, helping to keep you off the Medicaid program. Many of these

---

7   "Long-Term-Care Annuities to Go Tax Free," Diana Ransom, *Smart Money*, 2009.

riders will cover home health, assisted living or long-term care. I have seen a few where the benefit is a lifetime benefit and not restricted to a specific period of time. It is a win/win/win for both you, the government and the issuing company. These programs often do not require any medical examinations, which make them very attractive to those who have the potential for medical issues. These riders can be financial lifesavers. Another good thing about these riders is that if you end up not using the long-term care component, the money can be available for you to use for other things.

I have an example to share with you of a client we were able to help by attaching a health care rider to her financial accounts. I met this client several years ago, and she has MS (multiple sclerosis). She is one of those people who is always up and happy, a real pleasure to be around, and she has done a very good job of not letting this disease get the better of her. When I first met her, she had just retired and needed a walker to help her with her balance. She and her husband were not wealthy, so self-funding her long-term care needs would have been a real challenge. She was also not insurable, which presented another problem.

We anticipated that someday she might need to go into a care facility, so we opened an annuity and attached a health care rider that would help her fund her costs if she needed it. At my last meeting with her and her husband, she arrived in a wheelchair. The disease had robbed her of the ability to walk. Her husband is her primary caregiver, and they now want to sell their home and move into an assisted-living facility. They picked a nice place, but were concerned about their ability to pay the monthly costs. Fortunately, we had opened the annuity with the rider several years ago, and this particular annuity will pay a lifetime benefit. Without the rider, they may not have been able to cover the costs of the facility, but thanks to this account, they should be fine. The annuity has performed as prescribed, and in my opinion it has been a very smart investment.

This may not be representative of the experience of other clients and is not a guarantee of future performance or success.

As I mentioned previously, there are many different methods that you can use to help you pay for your long-term care needs. Take the time to learn about them, and consider incorporating one of these options into your financial plan. I personally believe that these health care riders can be one of the most important components of a well-balanced plan.

These insurance riders may make sense for many people, but unfortunately a lot of the public is unaware that they exist. If your advisor has not taken the time to discuss this important benefit, then it may be time to think about putting a new advisor on your team.

WHO DOES YOUR FINANCIAL ADVISOR REALLY WORK FOR, ANYWAY?

Who Does Your Financial Advisor Really Work for, Anyway?

Many of you may have financial advisors or stockbrokers who are "assisting" you with your finances. But who do they really work for? Are they working for you or the company that provides them with their offices and paychecks?

Many investors are taking unnecessary risks, being led down the wrong path by their financial advisors. Their portfolios may not be diversified properly, their finances may not be aligned with their goals and their fees and taxes may be high. In this section we will discuss how to know if the advice you are getting is in your best interest and not someone else's. We will also discuss how to find the right advice givers. If you are a disciplined and well-informed investor, financial markets will become your ally rather than your adversary.

SHOULD YOU JUST GO IT ALONE?

There are several key items that you need to consider when building your plan. Near the top of the list is whether you should do it yourself or seek professional help, and where you can find help.

There are a lot of do-it-yourselfers out there, and with the advent of the Internet, there is no shortage of investment advice. If you have the time and the fortitude, you should be able to do a good job on your own. Doing a professional's job on your own may involve spending hours researching companies and market theories. Many do-it-yourselfers are simply making their best guess based on an article they read. They would probably do significantly better if they had other members on their financial team, to share their ideas and help with investment decisions. This does not mean that you should not participate in your investment decisions; everyone should. But a qualified financial professional may help guide you in ways that bring significantly more value than what that the advisor costs. If you are paying your advisor a 1.0 to 1.5 percent fee and you do at least 1.5 percent better because of their advice, they have become essentially a free resource. They have brought you value that is at least equivalent to their fees.

If you are retired, you should be out enjoying your retirement. Sitting in front of a computer every day looking for the next great investment doesn't sound like the retirement that I have dreamed of. If you are still working and saving for retirement, you probably do not have the time or resources available to you that a financial professional may have. You should be focused on your job and keeping your income as high as possible and saving toward your retirement.

A qualified financial advisor should bring discipline and clarity to the investment process, and help you avoid traps that could impede your ability to realize your financial goals. Just make sure you are comfortable that he or she will bring you value above and beyond his or her costs.

I am sure most of you have spent a little time at the airport, maybe going to visit family for the holidays or to take a well-deserved vacation. When you get on the aircraft you will hear the flight attendants making their PA announcements. One of the most important is their "destination check." It sounds something like this: "Ladies and gentlemen, welcome aboard flight number 456; our flight today is to Atlanta [or wherever the flight is scheduled to go]." And they will then add, "If this is not your destination, now would be an excellent time to gather your belongings and deplane."

I have experienced several flights on which a passenger jumps up, realizing that he is on the wrong plane. He had boarded the plane, put away his belongings, relaxed, and was ready for an uneventful flight home. All of a sudden he went from relaxed and carefree to sudden panic: "I'm not going to Atlanta; don't close that door!"

So why did he get off the airplane? Well it's pretty obvious: The airplane was not going where he wanted to go. When you discover that you are in the wrong place and you are going somewhere that you don't want to go, you'd better get off the airplane and get on the right one.

My story about these passengers on the wrong plane is an analogy for life's journey. Sometimes you are on the right path and sometimes you are not. Soon the door will close and the plane will be airborne and you are committed. How long would it take you to get off the plane if it wasn't going to your destination? I imagine that once you discovered you were on the wrong plane, you would get off that plane pretty darn quick! What would happen if you did not realize you were on the wrong flight, and next thing you knew you were rolling up to the gate in the wrong city?

How does this relate to your finances? Getting to the right financial destination is extremely important. Once you recognize that you are going to the wrong destination, you need to make a change, and this may often mean finding a new advisor. I understand that sometimes change is difficult, but it is often necessary. It doesn't matter how many years you have been with your advisor, or maybe you are managing your own finances, if you are going down the wrong path, you may get into real trouble if you don't make a change. If you are not comfortable with your current destination, then maybe you need to "get off the plane" and find an advisor who can help you get where you are trying to go. Most of my clients are simply looking for financial stability and the confidence that the next stock market crash or correction will not ruin their retirement. They simply want consistent, reliable income that will last at least as long as they do, and a fighting chance to keep up with inflation. It is really not about hitting a home run in the stock market; most people just want financial security. There comes a time in your life when maybe you need to get off the financial roller coaster and start investing in a manner that allows you to sleep well at night. You can achieve confidence in your finances and your financial future; it just may require you to make a few changes and clearly define what is most important to you. Think about how much better you will sleep at night knowing that your finances are being well cared for.

HOW TO FIND AND HIRE THE BEST
ADVISOR FOR YOUR UNIQUE GOALS

Your finances, just like your health, are important. You need to arm yourself with the knowledge you need to find the "right advice givers." When you are interviewing new candidates to assist you with your finances, don't be afraid to ask them tough questions. You are interviewing a person who will not only assist you in managing something that is very important to you; you are interviewing a candidate for what will hopefully be a long-term relationship. You're the employer, so act the part. Ask advisors about their backgrounds, philosophies of investing, approach to risk, and how they get paid. If their answers make it seem like you won't be the one paying for their services, be wary. Nobody works for free, and if they tell you that they get paid by the companies they are recommending and not by you, you need to be even more cautious. Your relationship should be built on trust; your future advisor should be more than happy to tell you how he or she gets paid and even put whatever they tell you in writing.

First and foremost, work with an advisor that has to maintain a fiduciary standard to watch over your best interests, one that specializes in assisting retirees and those saving for retirement with their income needs and not an advisor that will simply work with anyone that walks in the door. My father was pretty good at a lot of things and he used to say, "He was a jack of all trades and a master of none." You want to work with the "specialist" and not the jack of all trades when it comes to something as important as your retirement income. There are advisors that are appropriate when you are in the accumulation phase of growing your assets, and then there are advisors that are most appropriate in the distribution phase when you are using your assets. Few advisors are truly good at both. As you test the waters to find the right financial advisor for you, you'll need to have a grasp on the areas in which you are seeking help. What do you want your future advisor to help you accomplish? Think about what concerns you the most about your current situation, and what your financial goals are for the future. The number one concern for many retirees is the possibility of outliving their assets, and this is a very real possibility in today's uncertain world. If you are drawing, or intend to draw, income from your portfolio, you need to work with an advisor that focuses on income planning.

If you currently have an advisor and you are evaluating whether change is in order, just ask yourself, "Do I feel confident that I will meet my financial goals doing what I am currently doing, or is there room for improvement?" No one wants to lose their hard earned money, take unnecessary risks, or outlive their savings. If your current advisor has not done a good job in addressing your needs or concerns, then I would suggest change might be in order. Too many advisors have become financial salespeople; you should work with someone who specializes in the area of your needs and will take the time to match their recommendations to your needs.

Since there will be costs associated with working with an advisor make sure you understand these costs and feel confident that the advisor will bring you more value than what they are charging. Once again if they tell you they are not charging you, or someone else is paying them, I would start looking for a new advisor. If the advisor charges 1.5 percent annually, then you should feel comfortable that you should do at least 1.5 percent better than you would have done without their help. It is important to understand that the value an advisor brings is not just in a better return; sometimes it is in their ability to identify weaknesses in your current plan that others may have overlooked, and provide strategies to help bring additional financial security.

You also may want to start building a relationship with an advisor you can trust, just in case you need their help in the future. What if one day you are unable to manage your own finances or you aren't able to watch over your current advisor. Do you feel confident that your current advisor can manage your finances and make the right decisions in the event that you are not able to actively participate with the decision process? Good advisors will maintain regular contact with their clients. They will call their clients in both the good times and the bad. Good advisors educate; they don't sell.

Here are some important things to consider when hiring the right advice giver:

Step 1: Is the advisor you are interviewing a fiduciary, and why is this important to you?

This may be one of the most important questions you can ask. One of the best ways for investors to realize their financial goals is to secure financial advice that is free of conflicts of interest by obtaining the services of an advisor that must hold themselves to a fiduciary standard. "Fiduciary" is a legal/financial term meaning an individual in a special position of trust and confidence who manages the assets of others with undivided loyalty, avoiding conflicts of interest.

Fiduciary responsibility = acting in your best interests.

In the investment world, Registered Investment Advisors (RIA) and Investment Advisor Representatives (IARs) are required to abide by a fiduciary standard; stockbrokers are not. RIAs and IARs are regulated under the Investment Advisers Act of 1940 and state securities laws, which requires them to act in the best interests of the investor.[1] This law requires that an advisor act solely in the best interest of the client, even if that interest is in conflict with the advisor's own financial interest. Investment advisors must disclose any conflict or potential conflict to the client prior to and throughout a business engagement. Investment advisors must adopt a code of ethics and fully disclose how they are compensated. Stockbrokers and large wire-house firms are currently exempt from the fiduciary standards under the Act. You would think that all financial professionals would be required to adhere to a common fiduciary standard, unfortunately this is not the case.

According to an article found on the Morningstar website titled, *Choosing the Best Financial Advisor,* by Steven Kelman and Gary

---

1   Registration as an investment advisor does not constitute an endorsement of the firm by securities regulators nor does it indicate that the advisor has attained a particular level of skill or ability.

Teelucksingh, "Be cautious with stockbrokers. They can be glorified salesmen hired by large wire-houses to sell proprietary mutual funds and stocks that the investment bank firm has promised corporations they will sell to investors. Proprietary products are those owned by the investment firm, and the brokers who sell these products get paid top commissions. In some cases, the investment may not be the most appropriate for the investor, but a lack of fiduciary standards does not require brokers to always do the right thing. With some wire-houses, it's all about quantity, not quality."[2]

A fiduciary is required to always act in his or her clients' best interest, and a broker is held to a very different standard. Physicians have a similar standard of ethics; why shouldn't your financial advisor? Make sure your new advisor is held to this high standard. Ask them if they are a fiduciary, and make this an important part of your decision.

Step 2: How should you pay your advisor?

Suppose you make an appointment and go see your doctor because you are not feeling well. After examining you and running a few tests, your physician writes you a prescription. Before you leave, you stop at the reception desk to pay your bill, but the receptionist tells you it isn't necessary, there is no charge for the doctor's visit. You go back to your physician and ask him or her why there is no charge. He responds, "Don't worry about it, I'm paid by the drug company." Just as with this hypothetical physician, an overwhelming majority of advisors receive payments and other incentives from outside sources

---

2 "Find the Right Financial Advisor," Steven Merkel, http://www.investo-pedia.com/articles/pf/07/rightadvisor.asp, April 10, 2009.

that can impair the objectivity of the advice they give clients. How an advisor is paid may affect the advice you get, so you may not want your advisor receiving some sort of incentive for selling you a particular account or financial product.

Generally, there are two ways an investment professional is paid: either through commissions or as a fee that is based on the assets under their management. Commissioned brokers typically get paid when they make changes to your portfolio. They earn a commission for buying and selling financial products, and ultimately the commission they receive does come from your account. For example, it is not uncommon for an investor to pay a 5 percent front-end load (commission) on an "A" share mutual fund, or annual fees (commissions) of 3 to 5 percent on Variable Annuities. These commissions can add up to a substantial amount of money. Consider this for a moment: if you own a Variable Annuity with a 3 percent annual fee and you have an average annual balance of $150,000 in your account, your annual fees will be approximately $4,500 per year. As I mentioned earlier, I believe costs matter and in my world, $4,500 in fees per year on a $150,000 account is high. If you have an average annual fee of about $4,500, and you own the account for let's say seven years, your total fees in this account can amount to as much as $30,000. I will suggest that there may be a more cost effective way to accomplish your goals without incurring these "high" fees. I have an issue with commissioned accounts, not just because of the high fees they may be charging, but also that the fees are often hidden in a wordy prospectus and not revealed on your statements. You may not see the fees on your statement, but they do exist and they can be substantial.

According to the article that appeared in *Morningstar*, "Choosing the Best Financial Advisor,"[3] "The commission paid on financial products varies according to the type of product, but generally the organization selling the product receives between 3 and 6 percent of the value of the product sold. In the case of mutual funds or insurance products, this amount may or may not be payable at once. An ongoing sales fee or trailer commission of 0.5 percent to 1 percent of the value of assets may be paid by many mutual funds."[4]

By paying your advisor through a fee agreement based on assets they are managing for you the enticement for your advisor to recommend buys and sells just to earn a commission should be gone. Another feature is that if you lose money, their fee will also decrease as a result. They will have an additional incentive to watch your money closely. Other fees may be applicable in your account such as 12b-1[5] fees and other internal expenses above and beyond the advisors management fee, so be sure to ask about any fees you may be paying.

It just does not make sense to me to pay for a service and not know the associated costs. You wouldn't buy a car without knowing what it costs; don't do it with your finances. Advisors, just like any other professional, do not work for free so make sure you know what they are charging and you feel comfortable with your fee arrangement. I have met with many investors who have insisted that they

---

3   www.morningstar.ca/globalhome/Industry/news.asp?articleid=877

4   *Choosing the Best Financial Advisor*, Steven G. Kelman and Gary Teelucksingh, International Thomas Publishing, 1999.

5   An annual marketing or distribution fee on a mutual fund. The 12b-1 fee is considered an operational expense and, as such, is included in a fund's expense ratio. It is generally between 0.25-1% (the maximum allowed) of a fund's net assets. The fee gets its name from a section in the Investment Company Act of 1940.

are not being charged a fee by their financial advisors or the firms they are investing with. They believed that their accounts are free, without any charges.

The fee-based model is quite common outside the investment business. For example, doctors and dentists are fee-for-service professionals. We would not want our physicians earning a commission from the medications they prescribe; it might bias the medical advice we would get. In the financial services arena, it seems that the majority of financial professionals are still being paid through commissions, although I am seeing that the fee-for-service model has steadily gained in popularity and usage.

Step 3: Ask yourself, how do you feel about the advice you are getting?

When you interview your advisor, he/she should take the time to educate you on your choices and present a plan of action that you feel comfortable with. You need to learn their approach to investing and have a good idea of how they will help you meet your financial goals. Ask yourself, "Do I feel comfortable with the advice I am getting?"

Your finances are important and making a decision about whom to trust is a big one. We have two very good tools to help us evaluate whether or not what we are hearing makes sense for our situation, a sort of internal radar system, *our brain and our heart*. Be sure what they are telling you makes sense (that's using the brain in the decision) and that you feel comfortable with the person and advice you are getting (that's your heart helping). If your internal "radar" is telling you something might be wrong, ask questions to resolve your concerns. If you don't feel comfortable after asking your questions, then it is probably time to move on and continue your search for the right advisor. Feeling comfortable with their investment style and the advice you are getting is critical to creating a healthy long-term relationship.

Step 4: Work with an advisor and not a "financial salesperson"!

An advisor's job is to advise and not to sell. All too often financial advisors are actually just glorified financial salespeople. A good advisor will take the time to learn about you and your concerns, educate you on your options, and present a formal written plan that addresses your specific situation. Too many so-called financial professionals just sell products like variable annuities or loaded mutual funds, and never take the time to really create a plan that addresses their clients' individual financial needs.

Picking a financial advisor is a lot like picking a physician. You want to develop a long-term relationship and be able to know that he or she will be there when you need them. When you go to a doctor because you are not feeling well the physician will ask you a series of questions, perhaps perform a few tests, and then form a diagnosis. Their diagnosis and treatment plan will be based on your personal symptoms and the doctor's years of experience. Your physician's job is to help keep you physically healthy. Now let's relate this to your financial advisor. His or her job is to help you protect your financial well-being. Much like a physician will help keep you *physically* healthy, your financial advisor's job is to help keep you *financially* healthy. Your financial advisor needs to ask questions, analyze your situation, develop a treatment plan (financial plan), and then educate you on his or her recommendations. If they do their job well, you will have confidence in the advice you are getting and feel comfortable looking to your advisor in times of need.

Step 5: Determine whether your advisor provides well-thought-out advice or is just a "Stock Jockey" or "Mutual Fund Picker."

Financial planning is complex, and navigating today's complicated markets is not a simple matter. To do it right, you need to consider a *multidisciplinary, holistic approach* to your finances. A holistic plan encompasses all family affairs: investments, objectives, risks, insurance, taxes, estate planning, retirement, asset protection, trusts, and wills. The traditional planning approach may miss one of these critical areas. In the financial services industry, some advisors place their entire focus on investments and forget that they are working with people, not just numbers.

Remember you are hiring your advisor to help you create financial security during your retirement; it is not about hitting a home run in the stock market. You want them to help you manage your risks, and risk management means addressing things like inflation, taxes, estate planning, and other forces that can derail your finances. This is where holistic advising comes in. Using a holistic approach to managing wealth puts together a team of professionals across many fields of expertise, evaluating every aspect of your financial world—from tax, retirement, and estate planning to charitable giving strategies to recommended asset allocations and investment solutions.

Simply having an advisor who is recommending a bunch of mutual funds or putting you in an advisor "managed" account is not enough. They need to be able to build a holistic plan that addresses all of the items that may affect your finances. If you are serious about reaching your financial goals and having your wealth serve you, then you should consider a holistic approach to your finances.

Step 6: Focus on the person, not the credentials.

It is not what they are called; it is what they do. You will encounter various labels: financial planners, wealth managers, portfolio managers, or maybe financial analysts. These labels are generic, and don't tell you much about a person's background, training, or approach to investing. So no matter what it says on the shingle, you need to find out precisely how an advisor proposes to help you to achieve your financial goals.

To learn more about professional designations you may want to read an article titled *Understanding Professional Designations* that The Financial Industry Regulatory Agency (FINRA) has made available on their website: http://apps.finra.org/DataDirectory/1/prodesignations.aspx. I have found from experience that too many designations are little more than sales tools and really don't relate to the true character and proficiency of the advisor.

Remember, you are hiring a person to help you manage your finances. The character of that person and their ability to provide you sound advice is more important than any credential they may have. Credentials sometimes can mask the true character of the individual; look beyond the credentials and evaluate the person.

Very simply put, some of the worst advisors I have met during my career have had a lot of fancy initials following their names, and some of the best did not.

Step 7: Keep in mind that you are unique, and your plan should be as well.

It can be very efficient and profitable for a financial company or an advisor to simply put you in a conservative or moderate fund with all of their other clients. Building model portfolios may be more efficient and profitable for the advisor, but is that what you really want? Do you really believe the advisor can address your needs by taking this approach? You are paying a fee to have your finances professionally managed and your concerns addressed; don't let an advisor just throw you in a conservative bucket with everyone else. Financial professionals are charging you a fee to help you with your money. Why not work with an advisor who will take the time to develop a plan for your specific situation and not just lump you in with the rest? It is what should be expected when you pay a fee. Don't accept anything else.

Step 8: Work with an advisor that specializes in your area of need and not a general practitioner.[6]

A specialist is a financial professional that has a specific focus for their practice such as retirement or income planning. A general practitioner is a financial professional that does not specialize or focus on any one area, but will generally work with anyone that walks in their door. Let's say you go to the doctor; he or she has been your family physician for years. You are scheduled for your annual physical. A week later you get called into the office to get the results. The doctor says, "I've got some good news and some bad news. The bad news is that your heart is all 'stopped up' and you are going to need open-heart surgery. So now you are probably wondering what the good news is? The good news," the doctor continues, "is that I have an opening in my schedule on Tuesday and we can do the surgery right here." What are you going to do? Are you going to let your general doctor—a family practitioner—conduct open-heart surgery on you

---

6   Specialist meaning a financial professional that specializes in a specific area such as retirement or income planning. A general practitioner meaning a financial professional that will work with almost any category or phase that the prospective client is in.

in the office? Probably not; most people will seek the opinion of a specialist, cardiologist or heart surgeon. Why? Because your heart is important to you and you will want to get the advice of a doctor who practices in heart-related care.

Your finances are no different. Work with an advisor who focuses in your areas of need. Ask your prospective advisor specifically who they work with and their area of focus. You do not want to work with someone who is all things to everyone.

Step 9: Be smart and trust your feelings.

You can tell a lot about a person when you meet face-to-face. Listen to the advice you are getting, make sure you feel comfortable with the advisor's approach to investing and his/her recommendations. Think of your meeting as an interview and you should leave with a good sense of how the advisor will manage your money and how they run their practice. You need to feel comfortable with both your advisor and the advice that they will provide.

> I recently sat with a gentleman, about 67 years old, who came in for an account review. He was very concerned with his investment results, for he had lost a lot of money. In fact, he was so concerned about his losses that he had gone back to work after being retired for several years. After talking with him, I saw that his concerns were right on and that his advisor was not doing a good job. We had several meetings to discuss his portfolio and his legitimate concerns. But when it came to leaving his advisor and going down a better path, he just couldn't make the change. When I explored this further, he told me his advisor took him golfing every month; he enjoyed the time with him and just couldn't change. I explained to him that his "green fees" were just too high. He was losing thousands of dollars, but his

advisor took him golfing monthly. I am not sure what happened to this gentleman when the market crashed just a few years ago, but he was certainly confused about the difference between professional help and friendship.

The biggest investment you will ever make is the one you make in yourself. You are the steward of your money, and you need to be actively involved in developing and monitoring your plan. To feel confident in your financial future you must be able to determine whether you are going down the right financial path. Take steps to find the right advisor and discuss your options. Learn to ask hard questions and to judge whether your finances are set up in your best interests, not someone else's.

INVESTING FOR A SECURE RETIREMENT: THE THREE INVESTMENT WORLDS

Investing for a More Secure Retirement: The Three Investment Worlds

"October…is one of the particularly dangerous months to invest in stocks. Other dangerous months are July, January, September, April, November, May, March, June, December, August, and February."

—*Mark Twain*

When building your financial plan there are several risks that you must address. Some of the key risks are the risk that inflation will erode the buying power of your money, the risk of outliving your money (longevity risk), and the risk of losing your money in the stock market (market risk). There is no such thing as a "safe" investment—only investments that are protected in some manner from certain types of risks. For example, a FDIC insured bank CD may be protected from stock market risk, but it certainly is not "safe" from the risk of inflation. Financial security comes from limiting or reducing your exposure to as many of the risks that can potentially derail your retirement. When addressing stock market risk, there is a saying that I believe is relevant for most investors, "As you get older you need to be safer with your money." This often means limiting your exposure to the stock market where you can lose your money in the next market downturn. How much money you should put at risk in the equities market is different for everyone, but I believe that you should never risk losing the money you need to live on. If you lost half of your life savings in the next market downturn how would you feel? I had a client tell me once, "I made it once; I don't want to have to make it twice." This makes a lot of sense, but then the question remains: If you are not investing the money you need to live on in the securities market, then where should it go? With guidance and good advice you can build a portfolio that will help provide for your future needs.

Mark Twain was right: October is a particularly dangerous month to invest in stocks, but so is the rest of the year. Jim Cramer, "Mr. Stock Market," tells us in his book *Jim Cramer's Real Money*[1] (New York: Simon & Schuster, 2009) that: "the stock market is a great place to grow your money. But because of the risks involved in such investments, transition some of your investments out of equities (or stocks) and into safer investments when you are in your 40s, and by the time you are in your 60s, the majority of your investments should be out of equities. The risk of the market is just too great, and the potential to earn money is limited by your time frame to invest." Isn't he telling us that as we get older we need to be safer with our money and reduce our exposure to stock market risk?

Ask yourself, is the stock market really that important to my retirement? The answer is different for everyone. Some people find the stock market exciting; others prefer to avoid risk as much as possible and not lose sleep over the thought of losing their money. The stock market can be a great place to help build wealth, but it certainly is not the place to preserve it. If the stock market is not right for you, or you simply don't want all of your money exposed to the trials and tribulations of the markets, fortunately you have other investment options. Think of the stock market as only one

---

1   *Jim Cramer's Real Money: Sane Investing in an Insane World*, James J. Cramer, New York: Simon & Schuster, 2009.

component of what should be a well-diversified plan, although, it is not suitable for everyone.

In the rest of this chapter, we will discuss your investment options and provide you with general ideas on where you may consider investing to help create a secure financial future. I believe there is an industry-wide bias to get you to invest the vast majority of your money in the securities markets, and I just don't believe that is appropriate for most investors, especially retirees or those approaching retirement. There is a certain amount of money you just cannot afford to lose, maybe you will need it to live on, and this money should not be put at risk! There is a very good formula that tells us that as we get older we need to be safer with our investments. You will hear people refer to this as the age one hundred rule. You simply take the number one hundred and subtract your age; this is the maximum percent of your portfolio that should be in risky investments. We will discuss this rule and how to apply it to your plan later in this chapter. Don't let your stockbroker tell you to put all of your money in the stock market and just ride out the storm. It may be in their best interest, but it is not their money; it is yours, and if they lose it, it will affect you and your family a whole lot more than your advisor.

THE PHASES OF MONEY

There are two primary phases of money: (1) the accumulation phase—your working years—when you are saving and building your nest egg for your retirement; and (2) the de-accumulation, or distribution, phase, where you begin to live off the fruits of your labor. In the accumulation phase, you are focused on earning money, paying your bills, educating your children, and saving for retirement. The stock market can be a very valuable tool during this phase of your life, and the longer you have to invest, the friendlier the stock market becomes. In the de-accumulation phase, you are using your money and one of the primary concerns is having the income you need to live comfortably in retirement. In this phase, you want to invest cautiously, create an income plan, and watch out for the things that can cause you to spend down your savings too fast. Will Rogers had a very good saying when it comes to investing during this phase of your life. He said, "I am more concerned about the *return of my money* than the *return on my money.*"

The focus of this book is saving and preparing for retirement, and is most applicable to people who are within ten to fifteen years of retirement (the Pre-Retirement Red Zone), or already retired. In retirement your financial strategy is about having the income you need to live and not running out!

THE KEY TO A GOOD FINANCIAL PLAN IS
ALIGNING YOUR FINANCES WITH YOUR GOALS

Is your goal simply to maintain your current quality of life or is there a need for improvement? Have you made enough money to live comfortably? Are you looking to just make a fair rate of return and not lose it? You need to think about your goals and make sure you are investing in a way that is not only comfortable for you, but will also give you the greatest possibility of successfully meeting those goals. Don't let the emotional aspect of investing take you down the wrong path. The two key emotions that seem to affect how we invest the most are fear and greed. These emotions may cause investors to make poor investment decisions regarding when to invest, or not invest, in the stock markets. These emotions may cause you to miss out on important opportunities or expose your money to unnecessary risks. Having a well-designed investment plan takes the emotions out of your investment decisions and helps ensure that you will feel financially secure, regardless of market conditions. Once you have the plan in place, you should only need to make minor adjustments as necessary. Even though I am suggesting that you do not let emotions drive your investment decisions, you must be comfortable with how you are investing. The goal is to feel comfortable with your investments and to be able to sleep well at night.

THE BUCKETING STRATEGY

Whether you are in retirement or in the pre-retirement red zone, the first step toward building your retirement plan is to define your needs and determine the right allocation of money to meet those needs or what I call "buckets." This bucketing strategy will help you determine the best investments to use based on your particular goals. If the goal is income, then we will create an income bucket and fund it with lower risk, cost-effective investments that may help to generate the income you need. If growth is the goal, a growth bucket is funded with cost-effective investments that have a good probability of meeting your growth expectations. Inflation, health care, and estate planning goals will be dealt with in the same manner. You build a bucket to address each one of these and fund it with the appropriate investments. This approach allows you to be very efficient and effective with your money, while providing you the opportunity to adjust each bucket easily to adapt to an ever-changing world.

We are now ready to discuss some of the investment choices you have to fund your "buckets." We will then go through an example of how to "put it all together" into a solid financial plan.

Graduation picture from Pilot Training Reese AFB.
T-38 Talon

Robert, his wife, Ana, and their two children, Sofia and Adam.

T-38 "Talons" flying formation
Robert flew this jet from 1984–1991

The Harwoods with Admiral McCraven

The Harwoods with Terry Bradshaw

Robert "On Air"

The Harwoods with Jay Leno

The Harwoods with Tampa Mayor Dick Greco

e i g h t

UNDERSTANDING YOUR INVESTMENT OPTIONS

Understanding Your Investment Options

We can take the investment world and divide it into three types of investments. Essentially there are three investment worlds for you to choose from. You can choose accounts that earn a fixed rate of interest, a market rate of return, or you can choose to earn a rate of interest that is linked to a market index.

INVESTMENTS THAT PAY A FIXED INTEREST RATE - THAT ARE PRINCIPAL PROTECTED BY THEIR ISSUERS

The first type of investment that we will discuss will be the most common investments available that earn a fixed interest rate and are principal protected. There are several investments that fall into this category, however the four most common are FDIC insured bank CDs, U.S. government treasuries, savings bonds, and fixed annuities (FA).[1] These investments typically earn a stated rate of interest, and at the end of their term, you will receive a return of your principal plus any interest earned. All four of these have several things in common. First, they are all vehicles for others to borrow your money. For example, a CD is a way for the bank to accumulate deposits so that they can redeploy that money in the form of mortgages or loans. They are borrowing your money in the form of a CD and then

---

1   These are not the only kinds of investments that provide a fixed interest rate; however, these are the types of investments that provide guarantees on principal investment.

lending it out in the form of a mortgage. The difference between what they are paying you on your CD and what they are receiving in interest on the mortgage is generally a "profit" for the bank. A treasury and a savings bond are vehicles where the government is borrowing your money and a fixed annuity is one of the ways the insurance company raises capital. All of these (bank CD's, government treasuries, savings bonds and fixed annuities) are similar in that they are all competing for your deposit. Another similarity is that the issuer of these investments is guaranteeing the "safety" of your money. In my opinion, none of these are good long-term investments. They just are not paying enough interest when you take into account inflation and taxes. Very simply put, these accounts are not at risk in the stock market and the principal is protected from losses in some manner, but none of them provide good prospects for real growth.

A MARKET RATE OF RETURN

Another option you have is to invest in the "markets" and earn a "market rate of return." These investments are invested in a market, like the stock, bond, or real estate market and are generally guaranteed against losses. These markets have cycles, and they can be really good for the investor or really bad; it just depends where you are in the market cycle. Generally, earning a market rate of return is better for long-term investors who are not dependent on their money to live, or younger investors who have more time to recover from market losses. The key to making money in the markets is time; you need to have the time to recover from any losses and the patience and time to let your money grow.

Some of the most common investments that earn a market rate of return are stocks, mutual funds, bonds, bond funds, ETFs (exchange-traded funds), real estate, and one of my least-liked investments, variable annuities. Because these investments are all driven by markets and they can go up and they can go down, they are not safe from losses, and they can lose money. However, if you have the time to recover from losses and the patience to ride out market cycles, they may provide the greatest opportunity for growth.

We have now discussed two key categories of accounts, those that earn a fixed interest rate with some sort of guarantee of the principal investment and investments that earn a market rate of return, like stocks, bonds, and mutual funds that can lose money. One group of investments is not affected by market declines but provides little or no opportunity for growth, and the other provides many opportunities for growth but involves a higher level of risk. You can lose principal when you invest in the markets. These were basically the choices our parents and grandparents had when making their investments decisions. They would buy stocks while working and accumulating wealth, and then use treasuries in retirement to provide security and income. Back then it was a different, and maybe simpler, world.

LINKED INTEREST INVESTMENTS[2]

Linked interest rate investments typically allow the account holder to earn interest based on a stock market index, but also

---

2 Guaranteed rate of return is subject to being held to maturity or for a surrender period, which may be several years. Subject to surrender fees and penalties if withdrawn early, this may be substantial. Rates may change without notice. Subject to market risk.

provide the principal protection associated with fixed interest rate investments. This means you are able to earn interest based on an external index, like the S&P 500[3] or the DJIA (Dow Jones Industrial Average), but are protected from losses if the index declines. For example, if the S&P 500 goes up, you may earn a portion of its gain in the form of interest, but if the S&P 500 goes down, you will not lose any of your principal. These linked accounts are typically structured investments and they often use some form of options to track an external index without exposing one's principal directly in the stock market. One of the investments that I like in this category that provides interest based on an exterior index (linked) is a type of FDIC insured Certificate of Deposit (CD). Rather than accepting a low fixed interest rate bank CD, you can choose CDs that earn interest based on market investments like stocks, indexes, or gold, but without the risk of losing money if the indexes value declines. These CDs are typically called "Indexed" or "Equity Linked" CDs and they can be a great way to attempt to earn a little extra money without exposing your principal to market risks. When I present this investment choice, people all too often were not aware that they could purchase an FDIC insured CD that pays them interest based on index returns like the S&P 500 or the DJIA, rather than a fixed rate. These variable rate CDs provide principal protection as well as the potential for some growth. These index CDs have evolved into pretty sophisticated investments, and you can now link them to gold, commodities, as well as foreign and U.S. markets. The choices are quite varied, and you can build a well-diversified portfolio without exposing your money to the downside risks of the market. Linked interest rate investments can offer the opportunity for growth as

---

3   Standard & Poor's, a division of McGraw-Hill.

well as the comfort of knowing your principal is protected from a bad stock market. I really like the linked accounts and believe that investors need to take the time to learn more about this category of investments. They may just provide you with the ability to grow your accounts and allow you to still sleep well at night not worrying about market conditions. Other "linked" accounts include TIPS and I-bonds that are linked to the rate of inflation (typically to CPI) and Fixed Annuities linked to a market index. These are often referred to as hybrid or Fixed Indexed Annuities.

THE HISTORY OF LINKED ACCOUNTS

Back in the mid 1990s the stock market took off like a rocket. Alan Greenspan called it "irrational exuberance"; everyone was flocking to the stock market and ignoring the risks of a possible correction. Investors pretty much ignored bank CDs and treasuries, since they could make 20 percent, 30 percent, or 40 percent a year in the stock market.

Since the banks still needed to raise funds (remember that CDs are a form of borrowing that the bank uses to access capital) they had to come up with a new idea. By linking the interest rates their CDs would earn, they were able to attract investors that wanted the security of principal protection, but did not want to give up the potential for growth that the stock market was offering.

Today, these are popular investments and there are a multitude of indexes you can choose from. For example, if you want to buy gold but you are afraid that gold prices will decrease, you could buy a CD linked to the price of gold. If gold prices go up, you earn some interest based on those gains, but if gold prices decline, you won't lose money. Linked CDs are a type of security and require a special license to sell them. You normally cannot buy these CDs from the teller at your bank. Equity linked CDs are only one of several choices you have in linked-interest-rate investments. Investments in this column will generally allow you to earn a portion of the gains of the external index without subjecting your money to loss. They typically have some form of guarantees and/or insurance against losses that are normally offered by the issuer of the accounts.[4] In light of the fact that we have gone through two major market corrections and extreme volatility over the last ten years, these linked rate investments have proved to be a good investment for many savvy investors.

> My wife had worked only a few years before we got married and she had amassed a small fortune in her 401(k) account. Her entire life savings at the time we got married was about $7,000. After we married, she quit working. She asked me to be her financial advisor, and as you can imagine, this scared me to death. Could you imagine what would happen if I lost one dollar of my wife's money? Not a risk I wanted to take but I really didn't have the choice to say "no" either. My solution: I invested her money in several CDs that were linked to the market, Equity Linked Certificates of Deposit. Her accounts grew nicely in the good years, but when the market crashed, guess how much money my wife lost in those CDs? None! Her account had pretty much doubled in value and the linked CDs were principal protected when the market crashed.
>
> At the time of this writing, I personally own CDs, treasuries, and fixed annuities, that all earn a linked interest rate. As an advisor, I practice what I preach and do not want to risk losing all my money,

---

4   Guarantees on annuities are based on the claims-paying ability of the issuing company.

> especially the money my wife and I will need to live on in retirement.
>
> This may not be representative of the experience of other clients and is not a guarantee of future performance or success.

In summary, you can get most of the fixed interest rate investments such as traditional bank CDs, fixed annuities, and treasuries in a linked version. They will typically, but not always, have some sort of limitation to access the funds inside of the account for a specified period of time—a penalty of some sort for an early or excess withdrawal from the account.

Here are the three investment worlds:

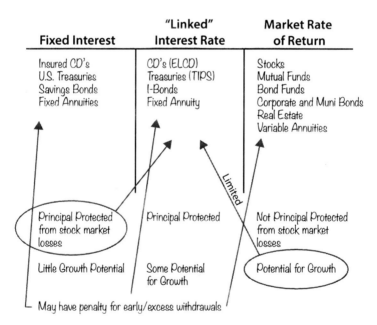

In the investment community there seems to be a bias on where they want you to invest your money. It seems that stockbrokers and mutual fund companies tend to want you to invest your money in the stock and equity markets. Banks typically want your money in the bank, because that is what is best for the bank. What should you do? Where should you invest? You should do what is best for you and your family and not worry about the banks or the big investment firms. It is not their money; it is yours! I am personally an advocate of using all three categories and diversifying your investments. I think it is a good idea to put your emergency money in the bank, where it is liquid and protected from loss. Put your growth money in the market, because it gives you the best opportunities for growth and a chance of keeping up with inflation; and put the money you don't want to lose—maybe you need it to live on—where it is principal-protected but maintains some opportunity for growth. (There may be some sort of penalty associated with an early or excess withdrawal as we see often with CDs and fixed annuities, so you want to make sure you maintain adequate liquidity.) If you want to keep some money as "safe" as possible you cannot just put it in the bank because you may lose money to the effects of inflation and you can not put it in the markets, because you can lose it there as well. I prefer to keep the money that I just can't afford to, or just don't want to, lose in the linked accounts where I have an opportunity for growth and the ability to maintain the integrity of principal protections. (Always take the time to read the prospectus and make sure you understand the pros and cons of any account before investing in it.) Balance is important, so the key is to diversify your investments and only use the investments that you are comfortable with.

You have great choices; unfortunately, many of your advisors may not be making their clients aware of them. If your advisor has not taken the time to explain to you your options you should ask yourself why. Is it because they didn't know about the various choices, or perhaps it wasn't really in their best interest to tell you about them? It is your money, not theirs; invest in a manner that is right for you.

AN ANNUITY PRIMER: IS AN ANNUITY RIGHT FOR YOU?

An Annuity Primer: Is an Annuity Right for You?

an·nu·i·ty/ahn(y)ōōitē/noun

1. *A fixed sum of money paid to someone each year, typically for the rest of his or her life.*

2. *A form of insurance or investment entitling the investor to a series of annual sums.*

Addressing the risk that retirees will outlive their assets is a growing challenge. According to a study by the Government Accountability Office (June 2007),[1] increased life expectancies and health care costs, coupled with a bad stock market, have intensified workers' concerns about how to manage their savings in retirement. The study indicated that retirees need to consider delaying taking Social Security benefits and add annuities to their portfolios in order to provide for dependable income in retirement. The report suggests that middle-income households that do not have traditional pensions large enough to cover their basic income needs should consider using a portion of their savings to purchase an income annuity. The study also points out that almost half of those near retirement are predicted to run out of money and will not be able to cover their basic expenses and uninsured health care costs. An annuity may be a valuable tool to keep your income flowing for what will hopefully be a long and fruitful retirement.

---

1 "Ensuring Income throughout Retirement Requires Difficult Choices," *GAO*, June 2007.

TYPES OF ANNUITIES

The four types of annuities are immediate, fixed, linked, and variable. Each can have an appropriate place in an investment portfolio when used properly. Annuities, like any other investment, may not be suitable for everyone, so you want to make sure you understand how they work and when or when not to use them.

IMMEDIATE ANNUITIES

This is an annuity and is most like a pension. You invest a lump sum of money in an immediate annuity and it provides a guaranteed income for the rest of your life, or for a specific period of time.[2] Immediate annuities that are bought for specific periods of time, (say for five or ten years) are called "period certain." Immediate annuities can also be purchased with a lifetime payout, which are called "lifetime" annuities. An immediate annuity with a lifetime payout means that payments stop when you die and typically no assets remain for your beneficiaries. Immediate annuities can provide a very good monthly income that is guaranteed by the issuing insurance company to last for your lifetime.

This type of annuity may be most appropriate for the individual who would buy a bumper sticker for their car that reads, "*I am spending my kids' inheritance.*" If you are not worried about what you leave for your children, immediate annuities can be an important part of your plan, but you want to buy them at the right time and at the right price. I do not like immediate annuities in low interest rate environments, since they will typically lock in their rates for your lifetime and will not adjust up when interest rates rise. Annuities in

---

2   Subject to the claims-paying ability of the insurance carrier.

general, regardless of whether they are fixed, variable, or indexed are considered long-term investments, so be sure to take the time to read the prospectus for the investments you are considering and make sure you discuss with the financial professional what it costs and how it fits into your financial plan.

FIXED ANNUITY

Like a bank certificate of deposit (CD), fixed annuities allow you to earn interest while protecting your principal.[3] Fixed annuities will have a stated interest rate—let's say 2 percent—and a term. During the term you will earn interest, and at the end of the term your full principal is returned, plus interest. The advantages of fixed annuities over bank CDs is that the interest earned in a fixed annuity is tax-deferred and, in some states, annuities are protected from creditors and lawsuits. Like CDs, if you cash your annuity in early, or take withdrawals above the allowed amount, a penalty may apply, so make sure you know what the rules are and that you are comfortable with the term on your annuity. Annuities will sometimes have terms longer than typical bank CDs and the penalties for early withdraw-als can be significant, so make sure you understand the terms and conditions of any investment you are considering before investing. An additional component of a fixed annuity is its ability to generate income. Fixed annuities can act a lot like pensions, providing consistent, reliable income for the life of the account holder through the use of withdrawals against the account.[4] In general, fixed annuities have

---

3   Subject to the claims-paying ability of the insurance carrier.

4   Withdrawals exceeding guaranteed rate of return will reduce principal which will affect future earnings.

a fine track record of safety and protection for an account holder's investment.

VARIABLE ANNUITIES[5]

Variable annuities are risk-bearing accounts and give the account holder the benefits of investing in securities, as well as all of the risks associated with investing in the markets. A variable annuity can lose money and may not be a secure investment. I have seen many cases where an advisor has told their clients that variable annuities are safe, that they cannot lose money, and sometimes even that they earn a fixed interest rate such as 6 to 7 percent each year. These statements are inaccurate. Variable annuities are securities investments, and typically investment results fluctuate based on the underlying port-folio's investment results. They are risk-bearing accounts, and your account value can go down; that is why financial advisors must be registered representatives as well as insurance licensed to sell them and why the word "variable" appears in their name. Another thing to be aware of are the fees and possible commissions that are associated with variable annuities. These fees are withdrawn from your account and will affect your investment returns. From my experience, when you add up all the fees in a variable annuity it is not unusual to see fees between 3 and 4 percent of the account's value every year. Over time, these fees can be substantial. Variable annuities, like all invest-ments, have a purpose, and they can benefit the right investor when

---

5 "Variable Annuities: Beyond the Hard Sell", FINRA, http://www.finra.org/Investors/ProtectYourself/InvestorAlerts/AnnuitiesAndInsurance/P005976.

used properly. "Most financial planning specialists, however, advise older adults to steer clear of these."[6]

A LITTLE MORE ABOUT FEES

There are normally five fees commonly associated with variable annuities:[7] (1) mortality insurance, (2) expenses, (3) administration, (4) riders (typically a fee for each rider), and (5) subaccounts. As mentioned earlier, I have seen many cases where a variable annuity was costing the account holder 3 to 4 percent per year of their account's value. This can become a significant amount of money, especially if you are in the account for a number of years. If you are considering one of these accounts, make sure you specifically ask about each one of these fees and make sure you are comfortable that the account you are buying is truly in your best interests and not someone else's. As a reminder, variable annuities are accounts that you may want to steer clear of since you may be able to find acceptable returns with less expense and volatility elsewhere.

FIXED LINKED ANNUITY, OR HYBRID ANNUITY[8]

Fixed indexed or linked annuities are principal-protected accounts[9] that provide the account holder with the potential to earn

---

6 "Making More Sense of Annuities," by Kelly Greene, http://online.wsj.com/article/SB1022771317695808440.html, June 2, 2002.

7 These fees are typically present in all annuities although the amount of each fee may vary greatly.

8 "Equity-Indexed Annuities—A Complex Choice", FINRA http://www.finra.org/Investors/ProtectYourself/InvestorAlerts/AnnuitiesAndInsurance/p010614, 9/13/2010.

9 Guarantees are based on the claims-paying ability of the issuing company.

a little more interest than bank CDs and fixed annuities, while still protecting principal from stock market related losses. These annuities offer some of the advantages of a fixed rate annuity in that the issuer provides assurances of principal protection as well as some of the advantages of a variable annuity by providing the account holder the potential for some growth. Like all annuities they also have the ability to provide an income stream that can be based on the account holder's lifetime or for a specified period of time.

The fixed linked annuity is designed for people who do not want to risk their principal to losses in the stock and equity markets, but would like to have a greater opportunity for growth than traditional savings vehicles. Suze Orman, in *Road to Wealth* (Riverhead Books, 2001), states that these types of accounts may be better suited for "individuals who want to play the stock market without risking their principal to losses."

Jack Marrion is a leading expert on this type of annuity. He writes in *Index Annuities: Power and the Protection* (Advantage Compendium, 2004), "People purchase an index annuity because they aren't satisfied with their returns from their CDs and fixed rate annuities, but don't have the time or temperament for the stock market. If you have sufficient time to recover from potential losses and the stomach for it, direct stock market investments should give you a higher return than an indexed annuity. However, if your time frame is too short to recover from a possible bad market or you simply don't like the idea of possibly losing principal, indexed annuities are used as an alternate savings vehicle to bank instruments, fixed rate annuities, bonds and bond mutual funds."

There are over a hundred different fixed linked annuities available on the market, and each has their own particular pros and cons. You can choose accounts that have a link to an individual index, like the S&P 500 or Dow Jones Industrial Average, or links to multiple indexes to include commodities, currencies, gold, and both foreign and U.S. Stock Market indexes.

If you are considering one of these accounts, make sure you are working with a financial professional who truly understands these accounts and can explain in plain English how the account works and any limitations related to the account. Additionally, make sure you are working with a competent and licensed financial advisor. Many insurance accounts like fixed, linked or indexed annuities can be sold by individuals that are not securities licensed, such as insurance only agents.   If you are considering one of these accounts I recommend that you look at what are called "10, 10, 10" policies. What this means is that you are able to withdraw up to 10% each year from the account without any sort of penalty from the company. This restriction on your withdrawals, known as the penalty period, will last no more than 10 years. Also 10, 10, 10 policies will limit the penalty associated with excess withdrawals to 10% or less.   Currently there are plenty of 10, 10, 10 accounts available that meet these criteria.

Below is a graphic showing a hypothetical linked fixed annuity that provides a link to the S&P 500. It compares its hypothetical performance to the index itself and a 3% compound interest rate.

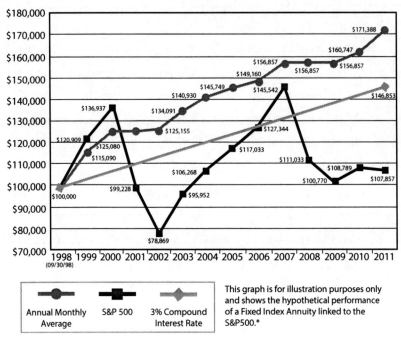

This graph is for illustration purposes only and shows the hypothetical performance of a Fixed Index Annuity linked to the S&P500.*

Annual Monthly Average	S&P 500	3% Compound Interest Rate

*The Standard & Poors "S&P500" are trademarks of McGraw Hill Companies, Inc.

If you are looking for safety of principal[10] with some potential growth as well as income guarantees, this type of annuity may be right for you.

IN SUMMARY

Annuities can be an important component of a well-constructed financial plan. Just make sure that you understand the annuity you choose and both its benefits as well as its costs. Make sure you work with a competent advisor who will explain to you both the pros and cons of the type of annuity you are considering. If there is something you don't understand about the investment or if something just doesn't make sense, don't be afraid to ask questions. Don't invest in

---

10 Guarantees on annuities is based on the claims paying ability of the issuing carrier.

anything, annuity or otherwise, until you feel comfortable that it is a good fit for you and your plan.

t e n

CREATING GUARANTEED INCOME

Creating Guaranteed Income

Will you need income from your investments during your retirement? Let's say your goal is simply to maintain your current standard of living throughout your retirement years and not let the "money snatchers" derail your retirement. You can consult a mortality table to determine, roughly, how many years you will need your money to last. According to the table if you have made it to your 65th birthday, you can expect to live to 85 years old. You perform a calculation and find that, together with your Social Security and your pension, you may have just enough savings to maintain your current standard of living until 85. What if you live longer, or inflation and taxes are a little higher than you planned for? What would you do if you ran short ten or fifteen years down the road? Will you be reduced to eking out an existence on Social Security alone? What if future investment returns are not what you anticipated at the start of your retirement? These are all valid questions that retirees and pre-retirees must consider, especially in today's economic environment.

Probability of Outliving Assets in Retirement

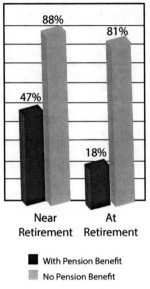

Americans for a Secure Retirement 2008

In a study by Ernst & Young LLP, "Retirement Vulnerabilities of New Retires: The Likelihood of Outliving Their Assets" (2008)[1] they estimated that more than three out of five middle-class retirees may expect to outlive their financial assets. This means that over 60 percent of retirees may go broke during their lifetimes.

The following is a recap of some of the key findings in this report:

1. More than three out of five middle-class new retirees can expect to outlive their financial assets;

2. Married couples are more likely to outlive their financial assets, due to longer joint life spans, than single households;

3. Single women have a much higher probability of outliving their assets than single men; and

---

1   "Retirement Vulnerability of New Retirees: The Likelihood of Outliving Their Assets," by Ernst & Young, July 2008.

4. Retirees who rely on Social Security as a key component of their income during retirement have an 81 percent chance of outliving their assets.

The study finds that retirees would be much better prepared to have a financially secure retirement if they have a guaranteed source of income beyond Social Security, such as annuities and defined benefit plans. The study found that retirees with these guaranteed sources of income are dramatically less likely to outlive their savings in retirement.

"At 65 years old, on average, you're going to need money until you're 85," says David Babbel, a risk-management professor at the Wharton School of the University of Pennsylvania, who co-wrote the paper, "Investing Your Lump Sum in Retirement,"[2] with Craig B. Merrill, an insurance and finance professor at Brigham Young University. "On average" means half of the people who achieve age 65 will live beyond age 85. To ensure that you have a stream of income that lasts for as long as you do generally requires an inordinately large beginning balance, and even then there is no guarantee that your account won't run dry during your lifetime. According to the two professors, an income annuity is the only asset class that most effectively addresses the risk of outliving your nest egg, because it generates a permanent stream of income unlike a typical nest egg of stocks, bonds, and cash. Meanwhile, the study notes, investors who place retirement wealth in mutual funds "are subject to greater risk, typically higher expenses, and returns that are unlikely to keep pace with annuity returns, when investment risk is taken into account." The best strategy, Professor Babbel says, "is to invest enough in an annuity early in retirement to cover basic fixed costs. That allows

2   "Investing Your Lump Sum at Retirement," David Babbel, Craig B. Merrill, Wharton Financial Institutions Center Policy Brief, August 14, 2007.

you to invest the remainder of your portfolio more aggressively. The risk of outliving your money, longevity risk, can be dealt with nicely with the right kind of low-cost annuity, but dealing with the risk of inflation is another story. This is an area where we want to invest in the stock market, although conservatively, to give us the ability to keep pace with inflation."

The Wharton study is telling us that the cost of not being able to cover your basic needs greatly exceeds the benefits you may receive from using the stock or bond markets (securities markets) as the driving force for your key income needs. "Not only do the guarantees provide a necessary level of security, but they are also a more cost-effective way to build your portfolio."

According to the study, a 65-year-old retiree who withdraws an inflation-adjusted $45,000 annually from a $1 million portfolio of stock and bond investments has about *a 25 percent chance of running out of money* before age 92. But if the retiree gets the same annual income by investing $600,000 in an income annuity and withdrawing the rest from $400,000 invested in stocks and bonds, the chance of running out of money drops significantly. What their study is telling us is that you may be able to generate more income from a smaller portfolio, $1 million if you are using a stock/bond portfolio vs. $600,000 in an income annuity, while greatly reducing your possibility of running out of money.

If you are seeking a "safer" income solution that is based on guarantees, you may want to consider using an immediate income annuity or a low-cost fixed or fixed linked annuity with a guaranteed income rider to cover your basic income needs. The guarantees in annuities are based on the claims-paying ability of the issuing company so you always want to work with a "high" rated company. A benefit of using a fixed annuity or fixed linked annuity (aka, fixed index annuity) instead of an immediate annuity is that they usually do not require annuitization, but can still provide a guaranteed minimum lifetime income steam through the use of a rider. This type of annuity is often called a "hybrid" annuity because it can serve more than one function. You can "attach" features like guaranteed income riders as well as other features. These hybrid annuities offer many of the advantages of a fixed linked annuity and an immediate annuity in one account. Insurance companies developed these hybrid annuities primarily for people who want the assurance of knowing their money will be available to create a consistent income stream and have the flexibility to choose when and how to use it. Products such as these have made the job of financial professionals a lot easier when creating income plans that are based on guarantees and not on the speculation or unknowns of stock and bond returns. They are designed primarily for people in the 45 to 80 age bracket who are focused on secure reliable income, either immediately or in the future.

Here is an example to show you how a hybrid annuity can be incorporated in an income-oriented financial plan. We will invest $250,000 in a linked-rate fixed annuity with a guaranteed income rider (a type of hybrid annuity). If you remember from our earlier explanation, the linked rate gives us upside potential while protecting the principal from losses. The worst that can happen is that in a given year, if the market declines, you may not earn any interest, but more important, you will not lose money.

What if the stock market goes down every year for the next ten years in a row? In this case you were lucky you protected your money, but, unfortunately, you did not make any interest either. To protect yourself from the possibility of zero growth due to a poor stock market, you can add a guarantee to your accounts so that your income withdrawals will grow over time regardless of index performance. These guarantees are provided through what is called an "income rider."

Let's say you invest in a hybrid annuity that has a guaranteed 7 percent compound growth rate for creating future income. If you invest $250,000 in this account, it will continue to grow each year by 7 percent compound interest until you decide to begin taking income from the account. Once you turn the income "on," the account switches from growth mode to paying out a prescribed amount of income each month. The account will provide you a minimum monthly income that is guaranteed for a specific period of time, normally your lifetime. If you are earning 7 percent each year and you are able to wait ten years to access the income from the account, the income account will double (Rule of 72) and you will have $500,000 to generate your lifetime income.

Through this example, you can see that these riders create a "personal pension," or guaranteed income, that will last as long as you do. Use of hybrid annuities with income riders are an excellent way to put money away for income needs while keeping your principal protected from market losses.

If you need your income sooner than ten years, your account will simply generate a smaller amount of income. Another great thing about these hybrid annuities is that their rates are guaranteed, so you can literally know exactly what your minimum guaranteed income will be in any one year. Since you are no longer subject to the peaks and valleys of the stock market, you can create a reliable income plan, and you can get off the investment roller coaster. Hybrid annuities can be the right choice for investors who are seeking consistent and reliable income from their investments.

> Some people think that if they buy a lifetime income annuity there will not be any money left for their children when they die. This is not the case with many of these types of hybrid annuities. You are simply taking withdrawals from your account while it is earning interest that is linked to a stock market index. When you die, any money left in your account will be left to your beneficiaries.
>
> Remember, whether you are buying an annuity or any other account make sure you take the time to read the prospectus and educate yourself on any fees, terms, or penalties for early withdrawal that may apply. Annuities in general will have some sort of term and limited liquidity feature so be sure to do your homework.

There are a lot of options when it comes to these hybrid income annuities, so make sure you seek the assistance of an advisor who truly understands these policies. In the next chapter, we will discuss how to incorporate hybrid annuities into your income plan. When used properly, they are an excellent financial tool, but make sure you understand the details about the annuity you are purchasing and that you are comfortable with how the annuity works and any rules or restrictions that may apply. Income riders with features similar to the ones I described in our example are available in both the linked hybrid annuities as well as variable annuities. The primary differences between the two are the risk to your principal and the costs of the annuities. I prefer using the fixed or linked hybrid annuities because of the lower costs and guarantees they provide. If you would like to read more about annuities in general or linked annuities in particular, Suze Orman has a very good chapter in *Road to Wealth* (Riverbend Books, 2001) that discusses these accounts.

Annuities serve a specific purpose, and they can be an integral and valuable tool under the right circumstances and for the right individual. I cannot stress strongly enough that with any investment, annuity or otherwise, you need to take the time to learn whether it is right for you. If you are thinking about purchasing an annuity, make sure the terms of the account are acceptable for your situation. You need to evaluate the term, guarantees, liquidity, fees, and expenses, as well as the other items that will be outlined in the annuity disclosure/prospectus.   If you are working with an advisor, ask them to put in writing their promises regarding the account you are considering including any fees that you will be required to pay. If they will not do this I would recommend that you consider finding a new advisor.

PUTTING IT ALL TOGETHER: AN INCOME PLAN THAT IS BUILT TO LAST

Putting It All Together: An Income Plan That Is Built to Last

In this book, I have discussed the many financial challenges that can possibly derail your retirement, as well as the investment tools to use to help keep them at bay. Also, I have introduced you to several of the investment choices available to build your plan. Essentially, you have a choice of investments that earn a fixed interest rate, investments that provide principal protection but allow you to earn interest linked to a market index, or you can invest directly in the equity markets where you have the greatest opportunities for gains along with all of the risks of loss. Now let's take what we have learned and put it all together into an income plan for retirement that's "built to last."

In this chapter, we are going to focus on building our plan and creating income that is based on guarantees. Retirees can choose to derive their income from investments such as stocks, bonds, and mutual funds or buy an annuity and create a personal pension, or create a composite of both. I like the idea of using a combination strategy. The stock market can be a great vehicle for growing your wealth, but not a great vehicle for preserving it. Certain annuities can be great for preserving your wealth and generating income, but they are generally not the best for growth. You have the three categories of investments you can use for building your plan: fixed interest rate accounts, linked interest rate accounts, and market based accounts. Use all three; the key is to determine the correct allocation of your funds into each type of account and to identify which investments within each category is best suited for your needs. This is what we are going to work on next. Let's build our plan.

We will build our plan using a bucketed model. If you recall a "bucket" is simply a way of identifying and allocating our funds for a specific need. For example, if we are targeting funds for immediate income then we will allocate an "immediate income bucket" and the funds in this bucket will be invested for this specific purpose. If the funds are for emergencies, then we will allocate a bucket for our emergency funds. In this exercise, we will create three primary buckets, one to generate income, another bucket for growth, and a third bucket for emergencies or unknowns. I have found that the most common buckets used when planning investments are current income, future income, survivorship income (to replace a pension or Social Security when a spouse passes away), inflation protection, growth, health care needs, and estate planning. Bucketing strategies have been used for many years by financial planning professionals and when done properly, will help to create a solid, efficient, and cost-effective portfolio. An additional benefit of a bucketed plan is that it is very easy to adapt and adjust, as things change in our lives and our world.

As we build our plan keep in mind that everyone is different, and for this reason no two financial plans should look alike. As a financial advisor and concerned professional, I listen to what my clients tell me and recommend a plan that specifically addresses their needs. The examples we develop in this book are simply for illustration purposes and are not intended to represent a complete plan that addresses all of retirees' financial needs. One of the primary lessons you should get from this book is not how to specifically build your own plan, but how to know whether your advisor has built a plan that is right for you.

Let's get started on building the plan. For this example I will use a hypothetical married couple, John who is 66 and Mary who is 65, and we will go through the process of building their plan. As you follow along, use your own numbers and build your plan. As I discuss their needs, think about yours. The first step is to determine what you want your investments to accomplish for you. What are your financial goals? John and Mary are already retired and their goal for their investments is to, "Provide income they need to support a good quality of life while in retirement."

The next step is to take a financial inventory. To do this, write down your sources of income: pensions, Social Security and the income you might be receiving from rental properties or from your other investments. Next, write down how much money you have in the bank and in investments such as stocks, bonds, mutual funds, or annuities. If you are married and your pension has less than 100 percent survivorship, write down the monthly income your spouse will get from your pension if you pass away first. The next thing you should note is how much monthly income you need each month to cover your current basic living expenses.

Our hypothetical couple John and Mary's financial inventory looks like this. John has a pension of $3,000 a month and if he passes away, Mary will receive $1,500 a month from this pension for her lifetime. The pension has a 50 percent survivorship on it. They have Social Security incomes of $1,700 a month for John and $800 for Mary and no other sources of income other than they take $1,500 each month from their investments. John and Mary have a total of $700,000 in investable assets and keep $50,000 in the bank. They do not have any life or long-term care insurance. They have determined that they will need $7,000 every month to meet their basic income needs.

Their specific issue is that they currently need an additional $1,500 a month of income from their portfolio, and if John dies before Mary they will have to replace half of his pension and all of her Social Security benefit. They do not have long-term care insurance, so we need to address this as well. They prefer that their income plan be "as safe as possible," but understand that they may have to accept some level of risk with part of their money to accomplish their goals. Here is a list of John and Mary's proposed goals:

1. Ensuring that they can draw consistent and reliable income from their portfolio of $1,500 a month for both of their lives in order to supplement their pension and Social Security.

2. The ability for their income to grow and keep pace with inflation.

3. Replacing income if John passes first, because Mary will lose half of his pension and all of her Social Security benefit.

4. The ability to cover some or all future long-term or home-health needs, because they do not have long-term care insurance.

5. Making sure that whatever money they don't use in their lifetimes goes to their children.

6. Maintaining their ability to have an active lifestyle and continue to travel.

> Your goals are the key to creating the right financial plan and picking the right investments. Whether you are investing for retirement or are already retired, your portfolio should be invested in a manner that will give you the highest probability of meeting your goals.

After you have taken your financial inventory, write down your goals for your investments. A common investment goal for many retirees and people looking forward to retirement is simply to "provide for a good quality of life in retirement." Other examples of goals may include leaving a legacy for your children when you pass away, or helping your children in a beneficial way while you are still alive.

Each one of your sub-goals will be important for you to enjoy your retirement and for you to have financial security. Simply missing just one of these can ruin your retirement. What is great about a bucketed plan is that once we break down our goals into smaller manageable pieces, we can then fund each bucket with specific investments that will provide you a high probability of success in meeting the goals. Hitting a home run in the stock market is not nearly as important as protecting your ability to accomplish these goals. In other words, if you are going to protect anything, it needs to be your ability to do the above six items (or sub-goals). If any one of those six items fail, you may be in trouble.

Now let's go back to our example with John and Mary. We have defined their income needs and broken down their retirement goal of "providing for a good quality of life in retirement" into smaller, more manageable pieces. We can now determine how much money we need in each one of their buckets.

To get this organized into a written plan, I like to use a specific format. I would invite you to take out a piece of paper and follow along.

Write *Investment Plan* at the top of a piece of paper, and just below *Investment Plan*, on the left-hand side, put the numbers 1, 2, and 3 vertically on the sheet. Indent each number slightly as shown below.

Investment Plan

1.

2.

3.

Next to number 1 write "Income," and to the right of Income, put a box. In the box write down the amount of monthly income you think you will need in retirement in that box. In our example, John and Mary need $7,000 per month. Note how much of this income will come from "guaranteed" sources, like Social Security, pensions or defined benefit plans, and how much you will need to withdraw from your savings. Above the box note the amount that will come from your savings and write, + inflation, next to it. In our example, John and Mary have $5,500 a month coming from their pension and Social Security and they are taking $1,500 a month from their investments to supplement their income needs.

Their plan will look like this.

Investment Plan for John and Mary

<$1,500/month*> + inflation

1. Income $7,000/month

*This is the amount they are taking from their investments each month.

2. Emergencies

3. Investments

Next to number 2 write "Emergencies" and next to it draw another box. Let us define your liquidity needs so we can establish an emergency account. This is money that will go into the bank or other investments, where it will be safe, insured, and easily accessible. At a minimum, keep enough money liquid to support your expenses for three to six months if you are working, and six months to a year if you are retired. In the above example, the hypothetical couple's income needs are $7,000 a month. Six months at $7,000 a month is $42,000, which is the minimum amount that should be earmarked for an emergency account. John and Mary have $50,000 in the bank, so we are good here. I put $50,000 in the box on row 2 "Emergency" money. Now take a moment to determine the amount of money you should keep in the bank and annotate this on your plan.

On the third line write "Investments" and write down the total amount of investable assets you have to support your needs throughout your retirement. In our example, John and Mary have $700,000. Write your assets in the box on line 3, "Investments." Your investable assets will normally be your total savings, including money markets, IRAs and other investment accounts, minus your emergency and checking accounts. This is probably the most critical part of the plan, since your investments will support your ability to have the income you need throughout your retirement.

Next, let's talk about your goals and what you want your investments to do for you. One of the big mistakes investors and their "professional" advisors make when picking investments is not clearly defining their goals for their investments. You must determine what you want your money to do for you to be able to identify the right investments. In other words, you cannot pick a good investment without first addressing what you want that investment to do for you! On your plan, underneath the box you created where you noted the amount of investable assets you have, write "goals" and then note your master goal. Underneath where you wrote your master goal, write the sub-goals that will be necessary for you to accomplish your main goal. Below is how our plan will look for John and Mary.

Investment Plan for John and Mary

<$1,500/month*> + inflation

1. *Income* | $7,000/month |

*This is the amount they are taking from their investments each month.

2. *Emergencies* | $50,000 |

3. *Investments* | $700,000 |

Sub-Goals

Goal: "Provide a good quality of life while in retirement."

1. Ensuring that they can draw consistent and reliable income from their portfolio of $1,500 a month for both their lives to supplement their pension and Social Security.
2. The ability for their income to grow and keep pace with inflation.
3. Replacing income if John passes first, because Mary will lose half of his pension and all of her Social Security benefit.
4. The ability to cover some or all future long-term or home-health needs, because they do not have long-term care insurance.
5. Making sure that whatever money they don't use in their lifetimes goes to their children.
6. Maintaining their ability to have an active lifestyle and continue to travel.

ALLOCATING YOUR INVESTMENTS

We are now well on our way to creating the foundation of a first-class financial plan. Before we start picking the actual investments for our plan, we will divide the investment world into one of two major categories. Simply put, investments fall into one of two categories: investments that involve risk of principal and investments that are protected in some manner. There are no "safe" investments. Help in achieving safety and financial security comes from a well-designed and diversified investment plan. I prefer to use the word "protected" versus "safe" to emphasize this point. "Protected investments" means that some aspect of the investment is guaranteed. For example, a bank CD is protected from stock market declines, but it is not safe from inflation. An annuity offers features that normally provide guaranteed income, but may not be safe from taxation. Gold is considered "protected" from the ravages of inflation, but can certainly lose value. Remember, although you can protect certain aspects of an investment, no investment is safe from *all* things.

As we get older, we need to be safer with our investments. If you are approaching retirement or are already retired, it is generally not advisable to risk all of your money in the stock or equities markets. The Rule of 100 is a "rule of thumb" in determining how much money you should have protected vs. in the riskier category. Remember, simply subtract your age from 100, and that is the highest percentage of your money that you should have in riskier investments. If you are 65, then you may want to keep 65 percent in the "protected" category and no more than 35 percent of your investments in the "riskier" category. If you are married, I suggest that you use the younger of your two ages for this calculation. The Rule of 100 is a good starting point for many investors, but can be modified since we are all different and we all have a different amount of savings and risk tolerances. If you feel you need to protect more than what the Rule of 100 formula would suggest, then do so. I personally believe that you should always protect the money you need to live on or are not willing to lose in the next market correction. If you have been a good saver and you can afford to put a little more in the riskier category, I believe this is fine, as long as you don't risk losing the money you need to live on. To review, the amount of funds that you should keep protected depends on how much money you need to keep safe for income, and how you feel about risk.

For a couple where the younger of the two is 65 a good starting point is to put 65% of the assets into "Protected" investments and only 35% in "Riskier" investments.

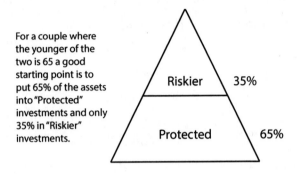

CURRENT INCOME

In our example we need to put aside enough money to provide for John and Mary's current income needs of $1,500 a month, as well as the income they may need in the future to replace 50 percent of John's pension and the smaller of their Social Securities. Unfortunately, when a married couple loses a spouse, they also lose one of the two Social Securities. The surviving spouse will get to keep the larger of the two Social Security checks but they will lose the smaller one. In John and Mary's situation this will mean a loss of $800 a month. If John pre-deceases Mary she will lose a total of $2,300 a month of income from John's pension and her Social Security combined. The $2,300 a month comes to $27,600 per year, which is quite a bit of money, and this potential problem needs to be addressed.

When determining how much money to put aside to protect the ability to create this replacement income, we must talk in terms of yields or withdrawal rates. A yield is an annual rate of interest earned in an account and a withdrawal rate is the annual rate of withdrawal that you take from your investments. For example, if you can generate a yield of 5 percent, or be able to have a guaranteed withdrawal rate from your accounts of 5 percent per year on a $200,000 account, you would receive $10,000 per year ($200,000 x 5%). In John and Mary's case we need to generate $1,500 a month from their portfolio. To determine the amount that we need to fund this income bucket, we divide the annual amount of income needed ($1,500 x 12 = $18,000) by the withdrawal rate (5%). This gives us the amount of money they will need to generate the required income. Take $18,000 and divide it by .05 (5%) and you will arrive at $360,000. This is the amount of money we need to put aside in order to provide for John and Mary's current income needs.

You may want to do the same calculation for yourself. The yields or withdrawal rates I recommend that you use for this calculation are as follows; if you are in your 60s, use a 5 percent rate, in your 70s use a 6 percent rate and if you are in your 80s, use a 7 percent rate. I am suggesting these withdrawal rates because this is the amount we can currently get guaranteed by using a fixed annuity or hybrid annuity with an income rider. I am using an annuity with an income rider for this example because I personally prefer to have all of my income needs guaranteed and not dependent on the whims of the stock or bond markets. This will also allow any money that John and Mary do not spend to be left to their children. Based on John and Mary's age, I can currently get an income rider that will provide a guaranteed 5 percent withdrawal rate from the account and it will guarantee[1] this income for both of their lives, similar to a joint pension. Income riders will provide income guarantees while you still maintain control of your money, since you have not annuitized your account.

---

[1] Guarantees on annuities are based on the claims-paying ability of the issuing company.

REPLACEMENT INCOME

Now we will do the same calculation for the replacement income that Mary may need if John passes away first. Remember, there were two types of income that we may need, current income and replacement. In this case Mary will need to replace $2,300 a month or an annualized amount of $27,600. If we assume, based on the life expectancy tables, that John lives into his mid-80s then we will need about $394,285 in an account when John passes to provide for Mary. The way I calculated this is I took the income need of $27,600 a year and divided it by the income factor (withdrawal rate) that is based on Mary's age at the time of John's passing, which I estimate to be 7 percent; she will be about 80 years old as well. Since we do not anticipate needing the $394,285 for about 20 years, we can invest a smaller amount of funds and let it grow to this amount. If we are able to grow our account by an average of 7 percent each year according to the Rule of 72, our money will double every ten years. (To use the rule of 72, simply take 72 divided by your expected interest rate and the number you get is the number of years it will take for your money to double.) Our initial investment will essentially double twice over the next twenty years if we are able to earn a consistent 7 percent each year. Currently there are fixed annuities with income riders that will guarantee that your income account value will grow by 7 percent a year each year you do not take income from the account. (It is like having a future pension and the pension will pay 7 percent more income each year we choose not to use it.) Knowing that we have a 7 percent compound interest rate each year the account sits in deferral (not taking income), we can estimate how much money we need to fund this account with to arrive at $394,285 in twenty years (John's life expectancy). We will need to put aside or allocate $98,571 to take care of this replacement income need for Mary.

INFLATION PROTECTION

Now that we have calculated our anticipated income needs and determined the amount we will need to fund our income buckets, let's look at inflation and how much we need to put aside for that bucket. To combat inflation you generally have two choices. You can invest in equities that you would expect to do well during times of inflation or set up additional income accounts that will provide a little extra income every few years. I personally prefer using the equities market, and I suggest targeting 30 percent of the monies you have allocated for income for this bucket. In John and Mary's case I have allocated $360,000+ $98,571 = $458,572 that is set aside for income purposes. Thirty percent of this number is $137,300 or approximately $140,000. For John and Mary, we will establish an account (bucket) with $140,000 and invest this money in equities to help offset the effect of inflation.

LONG-TERM CARE

One of the last remaining items that we need to address is how we will be dealing with long-term care related expenses. Rather than buying long-term care insurance, in this example, I want to address this issue by using a health care rider. If you remember from our previous discussion, many of the health care riders are attached to income annuities and will double your income if needed for a qualified health care expense. This will help to offset the costs of long-term care, although how much of a benefit you receive will depend directly on the amount of money you have invested in the account. My recommendation in this example is to attach the health care rider to both of the income accounts we set up for John and Mary: the immediate income account and the replacement income account. These riders are most typically associated with annuities and will potentially increase the monthly income from the accounts in the event that certain qualifications are met (such as losing two of six primary ADL's or spending a specified minimum period of time in a qualified care facility). In John and Mary's case the future income potential from their accounts are about $3,800 a month ($1,500 from the current income account and $2,300 from the replacement income account), so if either of them qualifies for this level of care required by the rider, then their income will potentially double from $3,800 a month to $7,600 month. This additional income can be used to offset the cost of their care.

There are several different income riders available on the market and they all can have different requirements for use, costs, limitations, and the benefits they will provide. I used a very simplified example in this case and recommend that if you want to learn more about these riders you consult a knowledgeable advisor. I personally like the riders since many of them do not require a physical examination and if you do not use the rider feature, your funds are still available to you for other things. The riders are designed to assist you with the cost of care and may not cover the entire costs of home health or nursing home care.

After we have allocated funds to our main buckets, there may be money left over. Any remaining funds can be invested in the securities market, or anywhere you feel comfortable. The stock market should give you the greatest opportunity for growth over the long term, but remember it also has the greatest amount of risk. You can also choose to put the additional funds in one of the principal protected accounts we discussed if you do not want to expose it to the risks of the equity markets. That will be your choice, and you should do what is most comfortable for you. The key is to fund your buckets to cover your basic needs and you can invest the additional funds in any of the three columns. This approach will help you assure that you will have the money you need to live on throughout your retirement.

The model I presented here is a very simple example. We normally build a much more sophisticated model for our clients with additional buckets that can improve the efficiency of the plan and ultimately help to save them money. A competent financial advisor will be able to help you create an efficient and cost effective model that addresses your specific needs. When you sit with your advisor, make sure that what they tell you makes sense. If they attempt to sell you on using a variable annuity in your plan, you may want to seek other advice. In my opinion, it would be hard to find a case where using a variable annuity would be either cost effective or efficient in an income model.

Here is what John and Mary's initial plan looks like:

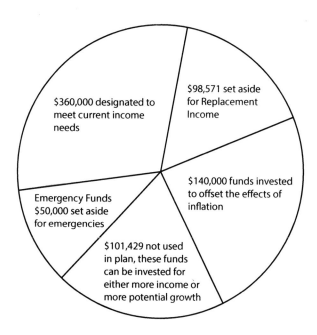

$360,000 designated to meet current income needs

$98,571 set aside for Replacement Income

$140,000 funds invested to offset the effects of inflation

Emergency Funds $50,000 set aside for emergencies

$101,429 not used in plan, these funds can be invested for either more income or more potential growth

ARE YOUR GUARDRAILS IN PLACE?

Are Your Guardrails in Place?

I live in Florida where we have several bridges that cross over large bodies of water. One of the largest and tallest is the Sunshine Skyway Bridge. This bridge is several miles long and stands about 180 feet tall at its highest point. Along the whole length of the bridge are guardrails to keep cars from going off the bridge. Why do they put guardrails on the highway and on bridges? The guardrails are for your protection; to keep you from going off the road. How would you feel about driving on the Sunshine Skyway Bridge if it didn't have guardrails? I for one wouldn't go near it!

Do you think it would be a good idea to put guardrails on your finances so you won't "go off the road"?

The fundamentals for financial success apply regardless of market conditions:

- Have funds in an emergency account set aside that will equal six months to one year of your annual expenses.
- Before you consider investing, make sure you have paid off all of your high-interest debt, like credit cards.
- Make sure you are not spending more than you make and have a budget.
- Have a long-term strategy for financial security.
- Work with a qualified financial advisor who will take the time to get to know you, understand your situation, and will help you achieve your long-term goals. Prosperity and financial security are a process, and you must have patience.

- Protect your income as best you can. You want to be able to feel comfortable, regardless of market conditions, that you will have the money you need to cover your basic living expenses.
- Do not panic when there is a bad day, or a series of bad days, in the equities market. If you have put aside the money you need to live on in protected accounts, you will be fine. Stick to your plan. If you don't have one, get one. It will help you sleep better at night!

I served as a pilot in the U.S. Air Force for almost ten years. I flew upside down more than once and spent time in the desert (we called it "the Sandbox"), the war in Iraq. Here is what I learned as a military pilot.

Always have a great team backing you up. You wouldn't want your jet mechanic or crew chief to be just okay. Each mission we flew had a goal, and we knew what to expect from the mission before we ever took off.

Your financial life is a lot like a military mission. You don't want it to be too exciting, and failure is not an option. You need to know where you are going. Always plan for the worst, and hope for the best! You are the steward of your financial future; make sure you have the right team backing you up, that you are working with the right type of advisor, and, most important, that you feel confident in the path you have chosen. If you fail, it is ultimately you who will pay the price.

People tend to be resistant to change, but in some cases change is necessary. If, after reading this book, you feel that there may be room for improvement in your financial plan, then go get the advice you need to get your finances on track. If your current advisor has not discussed the many important things we covered in this book, things such as TIPS, health care riders, linked accounts, and not risking too much of your money, then maybe it is time to find a new advisor. It may be that the advice you are getting is not suitable for your situation or you may have simply just "outgrown" your current advisor. In either case, no matter how difficult it might be for you to make a change, it may be necessary. Remember, when it comes to your financial security, don't settle for advice you are not comfortable with.

I hope you enjoyed this book and learned valuable lessons on the importance of finding the right advisor and how to know whether he or she is truly working in your best interests. The intention is to give you the knowledge to know if you are getting the right kind of advice from your advisors; and, if you don't have one, to show you the importance of getting a good advisor. I am not recommending that you go it alone, a good advisor can prove invaluable in today's turbulent markets, you just have to make sure you are comfortable with the advice you are getting.

Remember, it is not just about the money or hitting a home run in the equities markets, it is about creating financial security for yourself and your loved ones and having the confidence in your financial plan that it can weather the next market downturn.

Charts and additional supporting documents

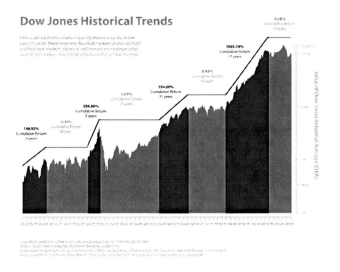

Dow Jones Historical Trends

From this chart we can see periods of growth in the market, followed by prolonged periods without real growth. The market tends to move in long cycles. I believe we are in a prolonged cycle where we will see little or no growth in the markets over the next several years, although there may be areas of growth, such as commodities.

Actuarial Life Table - Male   Period Life Table 2007

This life table is based on the mortality experience of a population during
a relatively short period of time. Here we present the 2007 period life table for
the Social Security area population. For this table, the period life expectancy at
a given age represents the average number of years of life remaining if a group
of persons at that age were to experience the mortality rates for 2007 over the
course of their remaining life.

Age	Years Remaining	Age	Years Remaining	Age	Years Remaining
35	42.5	61	20.2	87	4.9
36	41.5	62	19.4	88	4.6
37	40.6	63	18.7	89	4.2
38	39.7	64	17.9	90	3.9
39	38.8	65	17.2	91	3.6
40	37.8	66	16.5	92	3.4
41	36.9	67	15.8	93	3.2
42	36.0	68	15.1	94	2.9
43	35.1	69	14.4	95	2.8
44	34.2	70	13.7		
45	33.3	71	13.1		
46	32.5	72	12.4		
47	29.8	73	11.8		
48	30.7	74	11.2		
49	29.8	75	10.6		
50	29.0	76	10.0		
51	28.2	77	9.5		
52	27.3	78	8.9		
53	26.5	79	8.4		
54	25.7	80	7.9		
55	24.9	81	7.4		
56	24.1	82	6.9		
57	23.3	83	6.5		
58	22.5	84	6.1		
59	21.7	85	5.7		
60	20.9	86	5.3		

source: Social Security Life Expectancy Table, 2012,
http://www.ssa.gov/oact/STATS/table4c6.html

Actuarial Life Table - Female	Period Life Table 2007

This life table is based on the mortality experience of a population during a relatively short period of time. Here we present the 2007 period life table for the Social Security area population. For this table, the period life expectancy at a given age represents the average number of years of life remaining if a group of persons at that age were to experience the mortality rates for 2007 over the course of their remaining life.

Age	Years Remaining	Age	Years Remaining	Age	Years Remaining
35	46.7	61	23.1	87	5.9
36	45.7	62	22.3	88	5.5
37	44.8	63	21.5	89	5.1
38	43.8	64	20.7	90	4.7
39	42.9	65	19.9	91	4.4
40	41.9	66	19.1	92	4.0
41	41.0	67	18.3	93	3.8
42	40.0	68	17.6	94	3.5
43	39.1	69	16.8	95	3.3
44	38.2	70	16.1		
45	37.2	71	15.3		
46	36.3	72	14.6		
47	35.4	73	13.9		
48	34.5	74	13.2		
49	33.6	75	12.6		
50	32.7	76	11.9		
51	31.8	77	11.3		
52	30.9	78	10.6		
53	30.0	79	10.0		
54	29.1	80	9.4		
55	28.3	81	8.9		
56	27.4	82	8.3		
57	26.5	83	7.8		
58	25.7	84	7.3		
59	24.8	85	6.8		
60	24.0	86	6.3		

source: Social Security Life Expectancy Table, 2012,
http://www.ssa.gov/oact/STATS/table4c6.html

Table 4: State summary of retirement vulnerability

State	Probability of outliving their financial assets		% reduction in pre-retirement standard of living necessary to reduce failure rate to only 5%	
	Near retirees	New retirees	Near retirees	New retirees
Unit-ed State	74%	59%	-37%	-24%
Alabama	74%	60%	-37%	-24%
Alaska	73%	58%	-36%	-33%
Arizona	76%	64%	-41%	-29%
Arkansas	78%	67%	-42%	-30%
California	73%	59%	-37%	-25%
Colorado	77%	66%	-43%	-30%
Connecticut	77%	65%	-42%	-30%
Delaware	72%	58%	-36%	-23%
District of Columbia	60%	39%	-21%	-7%
Florida	75%	61%	-39%	-26%
Georgia	76%	64%	-41%	-28%
Hawaii	73%	59%	-37%	-25%
Idaho	73%	58%	-34%	-21%
Illinois	74%	59%	-36%	-24%
Indiana	77%	66%	-41%	-29%
Iowa	77%	66%	-42%	-30%
Kansa	75%	61%	-38%	-25%
Kentucky	74%	60%	-37%	-24%
Louisiana	73%	57%	-35%	-22%
Maine	76%	64%	-40%	-27%
Maryland	72%	55%	-33%	-20%
Massachusetts	73%	57%	-35%	-22%
Michigan	73%	57%	-35%	-22%
Minnesota	75%	62%	-39%	-27%
Mississippi	77%	66%	-40%	-28%

Table 4: State summary of retirement vulnerability

State	Probability of outliving their financial assets		% reduction in pre-retirement standard of living necessary to reduce failure rate to only 5%	
	Near retirees	New retirees	Near retirees	New retirees
Missouri	74%	59%	-36%	-23%
Montana	80%	72%	-47%	-35%
Nebraska	74%	58%	-34%	-21%
Nevada	77%	69%	-45%	-34%
New Hampshire	76%	65%	-41%	-29%
New Jersey	75%	62%	-40%	-27%
New Mexico	72%	54%	-32%	-19%
New York	70%	52%	-31%	-17%
North Carolina	73%	57%	-33%	-20%
North Dakota	74%	56%	-33%	-20%
Ohio	72%	55%	-32%	-19%
Oklahoma	77%	64%	-40%	-28%
Oregon	71%	54%	-32%	-19%
Pennsylvania	74%	59%	-36%	-23%
Rhode Island	71%	54%	-32%	-19%
South Carolina	74%	59%	-36%	-23%
South Dakota	79%	72%	-46%	-35%
Tennessee	75%	62%	-38%	-26%
Texas	74%	58%	-36%	-23%
Utah	71%	51%	-28%	-14%
Vermont	76%	64%	-40%	-27%
Virginia	74%	59%	-37%	-24%
Washington	74%	59%	-36%	-24%
West Virginia	78%	67%	-42%	-30%
Wisconsin	76%	62%	-39%	-26%
Wyoming	80%	72%	-46%	-35%

Source: Ernst & Young calculations.

Table 3: Retirement vulnerability of near retirees and new retirees

	Near retirement		At retirement	
	Probability of outliving their assets	% reduction in preretirement standard of living necessary to reduce failure rate to only 5%	probability of outliving their assets	% reduction in preretirement standard of living necessary to reduce failure rate to only 5%
	(1)	(2)	(3)	(4)
Marital status/gender				
Married	79%	-39%	65%	-26%
Single Male	57%	-30%	42%	-16%
Single Female	55%	-28%	38%	-14%
Employer pension coverage				
Covered	47%	-21%	18%	-8%
Uncovered	89%	-45%	81%	-32%
Income				
$50,000	74%	-36%	60%	-23%
$75,000	74%	-37%	61%	-27%
$100,000	75%	-41%	51%	-25%
Total	74%	-37%	59%	-24%

Source: Ernst & Young calculations. Group weights shown in Appendix Table A-2

Historical Higest Marginal Income Tax Rates

Year	Top Marginal Rate	Year	Top Marginal Rate	Year	Top Marginal Rate
1913	7.0%	1947	86.45%	1981	69.13%
1914	7.0%	1948	82.13%	1982	50.00%
1915	7.0%	1949	82.13%	1983	50.00%
1916	15.0%	1950	91.00%	1984	50.00%
1917	67.0%	1951	91.00%	1985	50.00%
1918	77.0%	1952	92.00%	1986	50.00%
1919	73.0%	1953	92.00%	1987	38.50%
1920	73.0%	1954	91.00%	1988	28.00%
1921	73.0%	1955	91.00%	1989	28.00%
1922	56.0%	1956	91.00%	1990	31.00%
1923	56.0%	1957	91.00%	1991	31.00%
1924	46.0%	1958	91.00%	1992	31.00%
1925	25.0%	1959	91.00%	1993	39.60%
1926	25.0%	1960	91.00%	1994	39.60%
1927	25.0%	1961	91.00%	1995	39.60%
1928	25.0%	1962	91.00%	1996	39.60%
1929	24.0%	1963	91.00%	1997	39.60%
1930	25.0%	1964	77.00%	1998	39.60%
1931	25.0%	1965	70.00%	1999	39.60%
1932	63.0%	1966	70.00%	2000	39.60%
1933	63.0%	1967	70.00%	2001	38.60%
1934	63.0%	1968	75.25%	2002	38.60%
1935	63.0%	1969	77.00%	2003	35.00%
1936	79.0%	1970	71.75%	2004	35.00%
1937	79.0%	1971	70.00%	2005	35.00%
1938	79.0%	1972	70.00%	2006	35.00%
1939	79.0%	1973	70.00%	2007	35.00%
1940	81.10%	1974	70.00%	2008	35.00%
1941	81.00%	1975	70.00%	2009	35.00%
1942	88.00%	1976	70.00%	2010	35.00%
1943	88.00%	1977	70.00%	2011	35.00%
1944	94.00%	1978	70.00%	2012	35.00%
1945	94.00%	1979	70.00%		
1946	86.45%	1980	70.00%		

Note: This table contains a number of simplifications and ignores a number of factors, such as a maximum tax on earned income of 50 percent when the top rate was 70 percent and the current increase in rates due to income-related reductions in value of itemized deductions. Perhaps most importantly, it ignores the large increase in percentage of returns that were subject to this top rate.

Sources: Eugene Steuerle, The Urban Institute; Joseph Pechman, Federal Tax Policy; Joint Committee on Taxation, Summary of Conference Agreement on the Jobs and Growth Tax Relief Reconciliation Act of 2003, JCX-54-03, May 22, 2003; IRS Revised Tax Rate Schedules

A Historical Look at Capital Gains Rates

	Individuals	Corporations
	Maximum capital gains rates	Maximum capital gains rates
1913-1921	same as regular rate	same as regular rate
1922-1933	12.5%	12.5%
1934-1935	17.7%*	13.75%
1936-1937	22.5%*	15.0%
1938-1941	15.0%	same as regular rate
1942-1951	25.0%	25.0%
1952-1953	26.0%	26.0%
1954	25.0%	26.0%
1955-1967	25.0%	25.0%
1968	26.9%	25.0%
1969	27.5%	25.0%
1970	30.2%	25.0%
1971	32.5%	25.0%
1972-1974	35.0%	25.0%
1975-1977	35.0%	30.0%
1978	33.8%	30.0%
1979	35.0%	30.0%
1980-1981 (June 9)	28.0%	28.0%
1981 (after June 9) - 1986	20.0%	28.0%
1987-1992	28.0%	34.0%
1993-1997 (May 6)	28.0%	35.0%
1997 (after May 6) - 2003 (May 5)	20.0%	35.0%
2003 (after May 5) - 2012	15.0%	35.0%

*Assumes 10-year holding period, 30% of gain recognized (sliding scale for exclusion based on holding period).

Please note: Tax law is complex. While an accurate representation of capital gains rate history, this chart may not reflect various factors (such as excess profit taxes, phase-ins, rates on special categories of gain and AMT) that could have affected capital gains taxes throughout the years.

SOURCE: CCH, 2012

Buyer's Guide to Fixed Deferred Annuities

Prepared By The National Association of Insurance Commissioners

Drafting Note: *The language of the Fixed Deferred Annuity Buyer's Guide is limited to that contained in the following pages, or to language approved by the commissioner. Companies may purchase personalized brochures from the NAIC or may request permission to reproduce the Buyer's Guide in their own type style and format. [The face page of the Fixed Deferred Annuity Buyer's Guide shall read as follows:] Prepared by the National Association of Insurance Commissioners The National Association of Insurance Commissioners is an association of state insurance regulatory officials. This association helps the various insurance departments to coordinate insurance laws for the benefit of all consumers. This guide does not endorse any company or policy. It is important that you understand the differences among various annuities so you can choose the kind that best fits your needs. This guide focuses on fixed deferred annuity contracts. There is, however, a brief description of variable annuities. If you're thinking of buying an equity-indexed annuity, an appendix to this guide will give you specific information. This Guide isn't meant to offer legal, financial or tax advice. You may want to consult independent advisors. At the end of this Guide are questions you should ask your agent or the company. Make sure you're satisfied with the answers before you buy.*

WHAT IS AN ANNUITY?

An annuity is a contract in which an insurance company makes a series of income payments at regular intervals in return for a premium or premiums you have paid. Annuities are most often bought for future retirement income. Only an annuity can pay an income that can be guaranteed to last as long as you live. An annuity is neither a life insurance nor a health insurance policy. It's not a savings account or a savings certificate. You shouldn't buy an annuity to reach short-term financial goals.

Your value in an annuity contract is the premiums you've paid, less any applicable charges, plus interest credited. The insurance company uses the value to figure the amount of most of the benefits that you can choose to receive from an annuity contract.

This guide explains how interest is credited as well as some typical charges and benefits of annuity contracts.

A deferred annuity has two parts or periods. During the accumulation period, the money you put into the annuity, less any applicable charges, earns interest. The earnings grow tax-deferred as long as you leave them in the annuity. During the second period, called the payout period, the company pays income to you or to someone you choose.

WHAT ARE THE DIFFERENT KINDS OF ANNUITIES?
This guide explains major differences in different kinds of annuities to help you understand how each might meet your needs. But look at the specific terms of an individual contract you're considering and the disclosure document you receive. If your annuity is being used to fund or provide benefits under a pension plan the benefits you get will depend on the terms of the plan. Contact your pension plan administrator for information.

This Buyer's Guide will focus on individual fixed deferred annuities.

Single Premium or Multiple Premium
You pay the insurance company only one payment for a single premium annuity. You make a series of payments for a multiple premium annuity. There are two kinds of multiple premium annuities. One kind is a flexible premium contract. Within set limits, you pay as much premium as you want, whenever you want. In the other kind, a scheduled premium annuity, the contract spells out your payments and how often you'll make them.

Immediate or Deferred
With an immediate annuity, income payments start no later than one year after you pay the premium. You usually pay for an immediate annuity with one payment. The income payments from a deferred annuity often start many years later. Deferred annuities have an accumulation period, which is the time between when you start paying premiums and when income payments start.

Fixed or Variable
• Fixed
During the accumulation period of a fixed deferred annuity, your money (less any applicable charges) earns interest at rates set by the insurance company or in a way spelled out in the annuity contract. The company guarantees that it will pay no less than a minimum rate of interest. During the payout period, the amount of each income payment to you is generally set when the payments start and will not change.
• Variable
During the accumulation period of a variable annuity the insurance company puts your premiums (less any applicable charges) into a separate account. You decide how the company will invest those premiums, depending on how much risk you want to take. You may put your premium into a stock, bond or other account, with no guarantees, or into a fixed account, with a minimum guaranteed interest. During the payout period of a
variable annuity, the amount of each income payment to you may be fixed (set at the beginning) or variable (changing with the value of the investments in the separate account).

HOW ARE THE INTEREST RATES SET FOR MY FIXED DEFERRED ANNUITY?

During the accumulation period, your money (less any applicable charges) earns interest at rates that change from time to time. **Usually, what these rates will be is entirely up to the insurance company.**
Current Interest Rate
The current rate is the rate the company decides to credit to your contract at a particular time. The company will guarantee it will not change for some time period.

• The *initial rate* is an interest rate the insurance company may credit for a set period of time after you first buy your annuity. The initial rate in some contracts may be higher than it will be later. This is often called a bonus rate.
• The *renewal rate* is the rate credited by the company after the end of the set time period. The contract tells how the company will set the renewal rate, which may be tied to an external reference or index.

Minimum Guaranteed Rate
The *minimum guaranteed interest rate* is the lowest rate your annuity will earn. This rate is stated in the contract.
Multiple Interest Rates
Some annuity contracts apply different interest rates to each premium you pay or to premiums you pay during different time periods. Other annuity contracts may have two or more accumulated values that fund different
benefit options. These accumulated values may use different interest rates. **You get only one of the accumulated values depending on which benefit you choose.**

WHAT CHARGES MAY BE SUBTRACTED FROM MY FIXED DEFERRED ANNUITY?

Most annuities have charges related to the cost of selling or servicing it. These charges may be subtracted directly from the contract value. Ask your agent or the company to describe the charges that apply to your annuity. Some examples of charges, fees and taxes are:

Surrender or Withdrawal Charges
If you need access to your money, you may be able to take all or part of the value out of your annuity at any time during the accumulation period. If you take out part of the value, you may pay a *withdrawal* charge. If you take out all of the value and surrender, or terminate, the annuity, you may pay a *surrender* charge. In either case, the company may figure the charge as a percentage of the value of the contract, of the premiums you've paid or of the amount you're withdrawing. The company may reduce or even eliminate the surrender charge after you've had the contract for a stated number of years. A company may waive the surrender charge when it pays a death benefit.

Some annuities have stated terms. When the term is up, the contract may automatically expire or renew. You're usually given a short period of time, called a *window*, to decide if you want to renew or surrender the annuity. If you surrender during the window, you won't have to pay surrender charges. If you renew, the surrender or withdrawal charges may start over. In some annuities, there is no charge if you surrender your contract when the company's current interest rate falls below a certain level. This may be called a *bail-out* option. In a multiple-premium annuity, the surrender charge may apply to each premium paid for a certain period of time. This may be called a *rolling* surrender or withdrawal charge. Some annuity contracts have a market value adjustment feature. If interest rates are different when you surrender your annuity than when you bought it, a *market value adjustment* may make the cash surrender value higher or lower. Since you and the insurance company share this risk, an annuity with a MVA feature may credit a higher rate than an annuity without that feature. Be sure to read the Tax Treatment section and ask your tax advisor for information about possible tax penalties on withdrawals. *Free Withdrawal* Your annuity may have a limited *free withdrawal* feature. That lets you make one or more withdrawals without a charge. The size of the free withdrawal is often limited to a set percentage of your contract value. If you make a larger withdrawal, you may pay withdrawal charges. You may lose any interest above the minimum guaranteed rate on the amount withdrawn. Some annuities waive withdrawal charges in certain situations, such as death, confinement in a nursing home or terminal illness.
Contract Fee A contract fee is a flat dollar amount charged either once or annually.

Transaction Fee A transaction fee is a charge per premium payment or other transaction.

Percentage of Premium Charge A percentage of premium charge is a charge deducted from each premium paid. The percentage may be lower after the contract has been in force for a certain number of years

or after total premiums paid have reached a certain amount.

Premium Tax Some states charge a tax on annuities. The insurance company pays this tax to the state.

The company may subtract the amount of the tax when you pay your premium, when you withdraw your contract value, when you start to receive income payments or when it pays a death benefit to your beneficiary.

WHAT ARE SOME FIXED DEFERRED ANNUITY CONTRACT BENEFITS?

Annuity Income Payments

One of the most important benefits of deferred annuities is your ability to use the value built up during the accumulation period to give you a lump sum payment or to make income payments during the payout period. Income payments are usually made monthly but you may choose to receive them less often. The size of income payments is based on the accumulated value in your annuity and the annuity's *benefit rate* in effect when

income payments start. The benefit rate usually depends on your age and sex, and the annuity payment option you choose. For example, you might choose payments that continue as long as you live, as long as your spouse lives or for a set number of years. There is a table of guaranteed benefit rates in each annuity contract. Most companies have current benefit rates as well. The company can change the current rates at any time,

but the *current* rates can never be less than the guaranteed benefit rates. When income payments start, the insurance company generally uses the benefit rate in effect at that time to figure the amount of your income payment.

Companies may offer various income payment options. You (the owner) or another person that you name may choose the option. The options are described here as if the payments are made to you.

• Life Only - The company pays income for your lifetime. It doesn't make any payments to anyone after you die. This payment option usually pays the highest income possible. You might choose it if you have no dependents, if you have taken care of them through other means or if the dependents have enough income of their own.

• Life Annuity with Period Certain - The company pays income for as long as you live and guarantees to make payments for a set number of years even if you die. This *period certain* is usually 10 or 20 years. If you live longer than the period certain, you'll continue to receive payments until you die. If you die during the period certain, your beneficiary gets regular payments for the rest of that period. If you die after the period certain, your beneficiary doesn't receive any payments from your annuity. Because the "period certain" is an added benefit, each income payment will be smaller than in a life-only option.

• Joint and Survivor - The company pays income as long as either you or your beneficiary lives. You may choose to decrease the amount of the payments after the first death. You may also be able to choose to have payments continue for a set length of time. Because the survivor feature is an added benefit, each income payment is smaller than in a life-only option.

Death Benefit

In some annuity contracts, the company may pay a death benefit to your beneficiary if you die before the income payments start. The most common death benefit is the contract value or the premiums paid, whichever is more.

Can My Annuity's VALUE BE DIFFERENT DEPENDING ON MY CHOICE OF Benefit?
While all deferred annuities offer a choice of benefits, some use different accumulated values to pay different benefits. For example, an annuity may use one value if annuity payments are for retirement benefits and a different value if the annuity is surrendered. As another example, an annuity may use one value for long-term care benefits and a different value if the annuity is surrendered. You can't receive more than one benefit at
the same time.

WHAT ABOUT THE TAX TREATMENT OF ANNUITIES?
Below is a general discussion about taxes and annuities. You should consult a professional tax advisor to discuss your individual tax situation. Under current federal law, annuities receive special tax treatment. Income tax on
annuities is deferred, which means you aren't taxed on the interest your money earns while it stays in the annuity. Tax-deferred accumulation isn't the same as tax-free accumulation. An advantage of tax deferral is that the tax bracket you're in when you receive annuity income payments may be lower than the one you're in during the accumulation period. You'll also be earning interest on the amount you would have paid in taxes during the accumulation period. Most states' tax laws on annuities follow the federal law. Part of the payments you receive from an annuity will be considered as a return of the premium you've paid. You won't have to pay taxes on that part. Another part of the payments is considered interest you've earned. You must pay taxes on the part that is
considered interest when you withdraw the money. You may also have to pay a 10% tax penalty if you withdraw the accumulation before age 59 1/2. The Internal Revenue Code also has rules about distributions after the death of a contract holder. Annuities used to fund certain employee pension benefit plans (those under Internal
Revenue Code Sections 401(a), 401(k), 403(b), 457 or 414) defer taxes on plan contributions as well as on interest or investment income. Within the limits set by the law, you can use pretax dollars to make payments to the annuity. When you take money out, it will be taxed. You can also use annuities to fund traditional and Roth IRAs under Internal Revenue Code Section 408. If you buy an annuity to fund an IRA, you'll receive a disclosure
statement describing the tax treatment.

WHAT IS A "FREE LOOK" PROVISION?
Many states have laws which give you a set number of days to look at the annuity contract after you buy it. If you decide during that time that you don't want the annuity, you can return the contract and get all your money back. This is often referred to as a free look or right to return period. The free look period should be prominently stated in your contract. Be sure to read your contract carefully during the free look period.

HOW DO I KNOW IF A FIXED DEFERRED ANNUITY IS RIGHT FOR ME?
The questions listed below may help you decide which type of annuity, if any, meets your retirement planning and financial needs. You should think about what your

goals are for the money you may put into the annuity. You need to think about how much risk you're willing to take with the money. Ask yourself:

• How much retirement income will I need in addition to what I will get from Social Security and my pension?

• Will I need that additional income only for myself or for myself and someone else?

• How long can I leave my money in the annuity?

• When will I need income payments?

• Does the annuity let me get money when I need it?

• Do I want a fixed annuity with a guaranteed interest rate and little or no risk of losing the principal?

• Do I want a variable annuity with the potential for higher earnings that aren't guaranteed and the possibility that I may risk losing principal?

• Or, am I somewhere in between and willing to take some risks with an equity indexed annuity?

WHAT QUESTIONS SHOULD I ASK MY AGENT OR THE COMPANY?

• Is this a single premium or multiple premium contract?

• Is this an equity-indexed annuity?

• What is the initial interest rate and how long is it guaranteed?

• Does the initial rate include a bonus rate and how much is the bonus?

• What is the guaranteed minimum interest rate?

• What renewal rate is the company crediting on annuity contracts of the same type that were issued last year?

• Are there withdrawal or surrender charges or penalties if I want to end my contract early and take out all of my money? How much are they?

• Can I get a partial withdrawal without paying surrender or other charges or losing interest?

• Does my annuity waive withdrawal charges for reasons such as death, confinement in a nursing home or terminal illness?

• Is there a market value adjustment (MVA) provision in my annuity?

• What other charges, if any, may be deducted from my premium or contract value?

• If I pick a shorter or longer payout period or surrender the annuity, will the accumulated value or the way interest is credited change?

• Is there a death benefit? How is it set? Can it change?

• What income payment options can I choose? Once I choose a payment option, can I change it?

FINAL POINTS TO CONSIDER

Before you decide to buy an annuity, you should review the contract. Terms and conditions of each annuity contract will vary. Ask yourself if, depending on your needs or age, this annuity is right for you. Taking money out of an annuity may mean you must pay taxes. Also, while it's sometimes possible to transfer the value of an older annuity into a new annuity, the new annuity may have a new schedule of charges that could mean new expenses you must pay directly or indirectly. You should understand the long-term nature of your purchase. Be sure you plan to keep an annuity long enough so that the charges don't take too much of the money you put in. Be sure you understand the effect of all charges. If you're buying an annuity to fund an IRA or other tax-deferred retirement program, be sure that you're eligible. Also, ask if there are any restrictions connected with the program. Remember that the quality of service that you can expect from the company and the agent is a very important factor in your decision.

When you receive your annuity contract, **READ IT CAREFULLY!!** Ask the agent and company for an explanation of anything you don't understand. Do this before any free look period ends. Compare information for similar contracts from several companies. Comparing products may help you make a better decision. If you have a specific question or can't get answers you need from the agent or company, contact your state insurance department.

APPENDIX I—EQUITY-INDEXED ANNUITIES
[Note: This appendix is not suitable for use in Massachusetts.]
This appendix to the Buyer's Guide for Fixed Deferred Annuities will focus on equity-indexed annuities. Like other types of fixed deferred annuities, equity-indexed annuities provide for annuity income payments, death benefits and tax-deferred accumulation. You should read the Buyer's Guide for general information about those features and about provisions such as withdrawal and surrender charges.

WHAT ARE EQUITY-INDEXED ANNUITIES?
An equity-indexed annuity is a fixed annuity, either immediate or deferred, that earns interest or provides benefits that are linked to an external equity reference or an equity index. The value of the index might be tied to a stock or other equity index. One of the most commonly used indices is Standard & Poor's 500 Composite Stock Price Index (the S&P 500), which is an equity index. The value of any index varies from day to day and is not predictable. When you buy an equity-indexed annuity you own an insurance contract. You are not buying shares of any stock or index. While immediate equity-indexed annuities may be available, this appendix will focus on deferred equity-indexed annuities.

HOW ARE THEY DIFFERENT FROM OTHER FIXED ANNUITIES?
An equity-indexed annuity is different from other fixed annuities because of the way it credits interest to your annuity's value. Some fixed annuities only credit interest calculated at a rate set in the contract. Other fixed annuities also credit interest at rates set from time to time by the insurance company. Equity-indexed
annuities credit interest using a formula based on changes in the index to which the annuity is linked. The formula decides how the additional interest, if any, is calculated and credited. How much additional interest you get and when you get it depends on the features of your particular annuity?
Your equity-indexed annuity, like other fixed annuities, also promises to pay a minimum interest rate. The rate that will be applied will not be less than this minimum guaranteed rate even if the index-linked interest rate is lower. The value of your annuity also will not drop below a guaranteed minimum. For example, many single premium contracts guarantee the minimum value will never be less than 90 percent of the premium paid, plus at least 3% in annual interest (less any partial withdrawals). The guaranteed value is the minimum amount available during a term for withdrawals, as well as for some annuitizations (see "Annuity Income Payments") and death benefits. The insurance company will adjust the value of the annuity at the end of each term to reflect any index increases.

WHAT ARE SOME EQUITY-INDEXED ANNUITY CONTRACT FEATURES?

Two features that have the greatest effect on the amount of additional interest that may be credited to an equity-indexed annuity are the indexing method and the participation rate. It is important to understand the features and how they work together. The following describes some other equity-indexed annuity features that affect the index-linked formula.

Indexing Method

The indexing method means the approach used to measure the amount of change, if any, in the index. Some of the most common indexing methods, which are explained more fully later on, include annual reset (ratcheting), high-water mark and point-to-point.

Term

The index term is the period over which index-linked interest is calculated; the interest is credited to your annuity at the end of a term. Terms are generally from one to ten years, with six or seven years being most common. Some annuities offer single terms while others offer multiple, consecutive terms. If your annuity has multiple terms, there will usually be a window at the end of each term, typically 30 days, during which you may withdraw your money without penalty. For installment premium annuities, the payment of each premium may begin a new term for that premium.

Participation Rate The participation rate decides how much of the increase in the index will be used to calculate index-linked interest. For example, if the calculated change in the index is 9% and the participation rate is 70%, the index-linked interest rate for your annuity will be 6.3% (9% x 70% = 6.3%). A company may set a different participation rate for newly issued annuities as often as each day. Therefore, the initial participation rate in your annuity will depend on when it is issued by the company. The company usually guarantees the participation rate for a specific period (from one year to the entire term). When that period is over, the company sets a new participation rate for the next period. Some annuities guarantee that the participation rate will never be set lower than a specified minimum or higher than a specified maximum.

Cap Rate or Cap

Some annuities may put an upper limit, or cap, on the index-linked interest rate. This is the maximum rate of interest the annuity will earn. In the example given above, if the contract has a 6% cap rate, 6%, and not 6.3%, would be credited. Not all annuities have a cap rate.

Floor on Equity Index-Linked Interest

The floor is the minimum index-linked interest rate you will earn. The most common floor is 0%. A 0% floor assures that even if the index decreases in value, the index-linked interest that you earn will be zero and not negative. As in the case of a cap, not all annuities have a stated floor on index-linked interest rates. But in all cases, your fixed annuity will have a minimum guaranteed value.

Averaging

In some annuities, the average of an index's value is used rather than the actual value of the index on a specified date. The index averaging may occur at the beginning, the end, or throughout the entire term of the annuity.

Interest Compounding

Some annuities pay simple interest during an index term. That means index linked interest is added to your original premium amount but does not compound during the term. Others pay compound interest during a term, which means that index-linked interest that has already been credited also earns interest in the

future. In either case, however, the interest earned in one term is usually compounded in the next.

Margin/Spread/Administrative Fee In some annuities, the index-linked interest rate is computed by subtracting a

specific percentage from any calculated change in the index. This percentage, sometimes referred to as the "margin," "spread," or "administrative fee," might be instead of, or in addition to, a participation rate. For example, if the calculated change in the index is 10%, your annuity might specify that 2.25% will be subtracted from the rate to determine the interest rate credited. In this example, the rate would be 7.75% (10% - 2.25% = 7.75%). In this example, the company subtracts the percentage only if the change in the index produces a positive

interest rate.

Vesting

Some annuities credit none of the index-linked interest or only part of it, if you take out all your money before the end of the term. The percentage that is vested, or credited, generally increases as the term comes closer to its end and is always 100% at the end of the term.

HOW DO THE COMMON INDEXING METHODS DIFFER?

Annual Reset

Index-linked interest, if any, is determined each year by comparing the index value at the end of the contract year with the index value at the start of the contract year. Interest is added to your annuity each year during the term.

High-Water Mark

The index-linked interest, if any, is decided by looking at the index value at various points during the term, usually the annual anniversaries of the date you bought the annuity. The interest is based on the difference between the highest index value and the index value at the start of the term. Interest is added to your annuity at the end of the term.

Low-Water Mark

The index-linked interest, if any, is determined by looking at the index value at various points during the term, usually the annual anniversaries of the date you bought the annuity. The interest is based on the difference between the index value at the end of the term and the lowest index value. Interest is added to your annuity at the end of the term.

Point-to-Point

The index-linked interest, if any, is based on the difference between the index value at the end of the term and the index value at the start of the term. Interest is added to your annuity at the end of the term.

WHAT ARE SOME OF THE FEATURES AND TRADE-OFFS OF DIFFERENT INDEXING METHODS?

Generally, equity-indexed annuities offer preset combinations of features. You may have to make trade-offs to get features you want in an annuity. This means the annuity you chose may also have features you don't want.

Features Trade-Offs
Annual Reset

Since the interest earned is "locked in" annually and the index value is "reset" at the end of each year, future decreases in the index will not affect the interest you have already earned. Therefore, your annuity using
the annual reset method may credit more interest than annuities using other methods when the index fluctuates up and down often during the term. This design is more likely than others to give you access to index-linked
interest before the term ends. Your annuity's participation rate may change each year and generally will be lower than that of other indexing methods. Also an annual reset design may use a cap or averaging to limit the total amount of interest you might earn each year.

High-Water Mark

Since interest is calculated using the highest value of the index on a contract anniversary during the term, this design may credit higher interest than some other designs if the index reaches a high point early or in the middle of the term, then drops off at the end of the term. Interest is not credited until the end of the term. In some annuities, if you surrender your annuity before the end of the term, you may not get index-linked interest for that term. In other annuities, you may receive index-linked interest, based on the highest anniversary value to date and the annuity's vesting schedule. Also, contracts with this design may have a lower participation rate than annuities using other designs or may use a cap to limit the total amount of interest you might earn.

Low-Water Mark

Since interest is calculated using the lowest value of the index prior to the end of the term, this design may credit higher interest than some other designs if the index reaches a low point early or in the middle of the term and then rises at the end of the term. Interest is not credited until the end of the term. With some annuities, if you surrender your annuity before the end of the term, you may not get index-linked interest for that term.

In other annuities, you may receive index linked interest based on a comparison of the lowest anniversary value to date with the index value at surrender and the annuity's vesting schedule. Also, contracts with this
design may have a lower participation rate than annuities using other designs or may use a cap to limit the total amount of interest you might earn.

Point-to-Point

Since interest cannot be calculated before the end of the term, use of this design may permit a higher participation rate than annuities using other designs. Since interest is not credited until the end of the term, typically six or seven years, you may not be able to get the index-linked interest until the end of the term.

WHAT IS THE IMPACT OF SOME OTHER EQUITY-INDEXED ANNUITY PRODUCT FEATURES?

Cap on Interest Earned

While a cap limits the amount of interest you might earn each year, annuities with this feature may have other product features you want, such as annual interest crediting or the ability to take partial withdrawals. Also, annuities that have a cap may have a higher participation rate.

Averaging at the beginning of a term protects you from buying your annuity at a high point, which would reduce the amount of interest you might earn. Averaging at the end of the term protects you against severe declines in the index and losing index-linked interest as a result. On the other hand, averaging may reduce the amount of index-linked interest you earn when the index rises either near the start or at the end of the term.

Participation Rate

The participation rate may vary greatly from one annuity to another and from time to time within a particular annuity. Therefore, it is important for you to know how your annuity's participation rate works with the indexing method. A high participation rate may be offset by other features, such as simple interest, averaging, or a point-to-point indexing method. On the other hand, an insurance company may offset a lower participation rate by also offering a feature such as an annual reset indexing method.

Interest Compounding

It is important for you to know whether your annuity pays compound or simple interest during a term. While you may earn less from an annuity that pays simple interest, it may have other features you want, such as a higher participation rate.

WHAT WILL IT COST ME TO TAKE MY MONEY OUT BEFORE THE END OF THE TERM?

In addition to the information discussed in this Buyer's Guide about surrender and withdrawal charges and free withdrawals, there are additional considerations for equity-indexed annuities. Some annuities credit none of the index-linked interest or only part of it if you take out money before the end of the term. The percentage that is vested, or credited, generally increases as the term comes closer to its end and is always 100% at the end of the term.

ARE DIVIDENDS INCLUDED IN THE INDEX?

Depending on the index used, stock dividends may or may not be included in the index's value. For example, the S&P 500 is a stock price index and only considers the prices of stocks. It does not recognize any dividends paid on those stocks.

HOW DO I KNOW IF AN EQUITY-INDEXED ANNUITY IS RIGHT FOR ME? The

questions listed below may help you decide which type of annuity, if any, meets your retirement planning and financial needs. You should consider what your goals are for the money you may put into the annuity. You need to think about how much risk you're willing to take with the money. Ask yourself:

Am I interested in a variable annuity with the potential for higher earnings that are not guaranteed and willing to risk losing the principal?

Is a guaranteed interest rate more important to me, with little or no risk of losing the principal?

Or, am I somewhere in between these two extremes and willing to take some risks?

HOW DO I KNOW WHICH EQUITY-INDEXED ANNUITY IS BEST FOR ME?

As with any other insurance product, you must carefully consider your own personal situation and how you feel about the choices available. No single annuity design may have all the features you want. It is important to understand the features and trade-offs available so you can choose the annuity that is right for you. Keep in mind that it may be misleading to compare one annuity to another unless you compare all the other features of each annuity. You must decide for yourself what combination of features makes the most sense for you. Also remember that it is not possible to predict the future behavior of an index.

QUESTIONS YOU SHOULD ASK YOUR AGENT OR THE COMPANY

You should ask the following questions about equity-indexed annuities in addition to the questions in the Buyer's Guide to Fixed Deferred Annuities.

• How long is the term?

• What is the guaranteed minimum interest rate?

• What is the participation rate? For how long is the participation rate guaranteed?

• Is there a minimum participation rate?

• Does my contract have an interest rate cap? What is it?

• Does my contract have an interest rate floor? What is it?

• Is interest rate averaging used? How does it work?

• Is interest compounded during a term? • Is there a margin, spread, or administrative fee? Is that in addition to or instead of a participation rate?

• What indexing method is used in my contract?

• What are the surrender charges or penalties if I want to end my contract early and take out all of my money?

• Can I get a partial withdrawal without paying charges or losing interest?

Does my contract have vesting? If so, what is the rate of vesting?

Final Points to Consider

Remember to read your annuity contract carefully when you receive it. Ask your agent or insurance company to explain anything you don't understand. If you have a specific complaint or can't get answers you need from the agent or company, contact your state insurance department.

How can you use this book?

MOTIVATE

EDUCATE

THANK

INSPIRE

PROMOTE

CONNECT

Why have a custom version of *Investing for Retirement*?

- Build personal bonds with customers, prospects, employees, donors, and key constituencies
- Develop a long-lasting reminder of your event, milestone, or celebration
- Provide a keepsake that inspires change in behavior and change in lives
- Deliver the ultimate "thank you" gift that remains on coffee tables and bookshelves
- Generate the "wow" factor

Books are thoughtful gifts that provide a genuine sentiment that other promotional items cannot express. They promote employee discussions and interaction, reinforce an event's meaning or location, and they make a lasting impression. Use your book to say "Thank You" and show people that you care.

Investing for Retirement is available in bulk quantities and in customized versions at special discounts for corporate, institutional, and educational purposes. To learn more please contact our Special Sales team at:

1.866.775.1696 • sales@advantageww.com • www.AdvantageSpecialSales.com

CPSIA information can be obtained at www.ICGtesting.com
Printed in the USA
LVOW120329020513

331730LV00001B/4/P